The lazy winner

To my mum and dad, who have discovered the joys of international travel late in life; hopefully this book will help compensate for the loss of my inheritance through these frivolous expenditures.

And to my brother, Justin, who isn't helping matters at all by living in South Africa.

Love you all.

Peter Taylor

The lazy
winner

How to do more with less effort and succeed in your work and personal life without rushing around like a headless chicken or putting in 100 hour weeks

infinite ideas

First published in 2011 by
Infinite Ideas Limited
36 St Giles
Oxford
OX1 3LD
United Kingdom
www.infideas.com

A CIP catalogue record for this book is available from the British Library

ISBN 978-1-906821-89-0

Cover designed by Darren Hayball
Text designed and typeset by Nicki Averill
Printed and bound in Great Britain

Contents

Acknowledgements

There seem to be a lot of people out there who like the idea of being 'lazy' but in a 'productive' way, so I want to thank everyone who has supported me and encouraged me so far. That said, you can only blame yourselves that there is now a whole new book on the subject in the marketplace.

As usual when such a book is born there will be a long list of people that I should thank but applying my own principles of 'laziness' I will just say that 'you know who you are' and that I am 'enthusiastically grateful' to all of you. And as this is not an Oscar speech I don't even have to mention the enormous contribution my goldfish made.

There, easily done and without running the risk of missing someone off the list.

I hope that you enjoy the book and I do really appreciate everyone who has had the slightest influence or impact on me over the years; without you who knows what success I might have actually enjoyed.

Thanks to all of you and be 'lazy'.

Peter

Foreword

We all need a little help in our lives, I know I do, and sometimes you just reach out and grab on to a lifeline when the opportunity arrives.

For me, it arrived one lunch time when I was out and about attempting to enjoy some downtime and yet stressed by what was waiting for me back at the office.

I happened upon *The lazy winner* and, despite my reservations about self-help books in general, I was drawn by the fact that the book seemed honest and easy to read. Indeed it starts by giving the would-be reader the opportunity to reconsider the potential purchase and suggests that they should understand exactly what it can and can't do for them.

For me it led to a series of small changes that have resulted in a big change in my life.

For me becoming a lazy winner has become a reality.

I am sure it can do the same for you.

Nigel (You'll hear more about him later on.)

Decision

'Ambition is a poor excuse for not having sense enough to be lazy.'

Charlie McCarthy (Edgar Bergen)

Are you sure you want to read this book?

Stop reading this book now!

Well actually I mean stop reading this book at the end of this chapter and then follow the instructions explicitly before you continue. Trust me on this one, I'm an author, and it really is in your best interests. Clear? Good!

So let's start with a simple summary of what lies ahead of you in this book and then take a quick test to see if it is worth your while investing your time (and money) further.

What is it all about?

The lazy winner is for anyone who simply wants to do more with less effort and succeed in their work and personal life without rushing around like a headless chicken or putting in100 hour weeks. We are all too good to put our personal life and careers and work–life balance at risk by working too hard! Equally we can't head off in the opposite direction and ignore the 'work' part of the equation while focusing our time and effort solely on the 'life' part. That is not a work–life balance at all and, unless you are already wealthy enough to go for just a life–life balance[1] then you do need to come up with a real 'balance' that applies to you.

---

1. If this is the case and you are just idly reading this book on your private yacht while waiting for the caviar to be served please send all donations through my website www.thelazywinner.com – thank you – all major credit cards accepted, naturally.

You are just too good to fail at what you do and I want to help you get even better at succeeding in what you do in the future.

The lazy winner builds on the concept of 'productive laziness' which encourages people to apply more thought before leaping into action and throwing effort at a problem or task. There are much better ways to progress in work and in life. I mean, what is the point in rushing around like busy bees all of the time and yet looking back at the end of the day and wondering what it was all about and what you actually achieved.

With a different approach to planning you can ensure that you are one of the lazy winners and achieve success in what you do at work and in life – achieving more impressive results with the minimum of effort.

What is it not about?

I want you to make the right decision here about this book and the outline of what it aims to do will, hopefully, put you on the right path. Equally I should be clear about what this book isn't about and what it won't give you.

There are hundreds of self-help books out there that will promise to help you 'get paid more, laid more and live a longer happier life'. This isn't one of them (I may have just lost out on a million sales with that statement but I have to be honest[2]).

What I do believe is that by adopting a few simple rules in your life you can make changes that can be quite significant, depending upon your starting point of course, and what your expectations are of such change.

---

2. The publishers would like to point out that it may well be possible to achieve everything that other self-help books offer so you might like to buy the book anyway on the off chance that this happens – but no guarantee is provided. (A search on Amazon.com for 'self-help' books currently shows a staggering 129,325 books with 'self-help' in the title or as the contents tag. It is also said that the self-help market in 2010 was valued at just under $12 billion.) Note: Perhaps the next book in the series will be *The happy lazy book of getting laid and paid more.*

What this book is then is a roadmap, a route planner, a step-by-step progress plan, to guide you on your way to achieving some level of 'productive laziness'. And that is an important thing to understand. You don't have to go for the 'big bang'[3] approach and you don't have to do 100% of what I suggest to achieve some benefits. I believe that you will achieve some advantage at each stage – small incremental gains as each lesson is learned and applied.

Again, many self-help books only work if you entirely immerse yourself in what they have to say and then adopt all the advice to the maximum. And when you fail to make any significant changes it will be your fault for not doing it all properly and thoroughly enough.

This book is not like that.

So, should you read this book?

You need to ask yourself some questions before you make up your mind.

What happens when you get involved in something? Do you get carried along in the excitement of it all, caught up in the rush, or just accept everything that heads your way with a spirit of fatalism? Or do you ever hold back and ask yourself:

- Do I want to do this piece of work, job or task? Even if I do want to do it, do I need to do it?
- Is the potential result or outcome worth my effort?
- Do I have to do it myself?
- If you have to do to it then what is the shortest path to the point of success?
- What exactly is that point of success and at what stage will you just be wasting your time?

---

3. The 'big bang' relates to the cosmological theory that the start of the cosmos happened at one moment in time. This is also the case with the big bang adoption type where a new system is adopted on one date (often applicable in software implementations).

If you get a clean run of 'Yes I do that' across all five questions then put your purse or wallet away and go buy something else.[4] You are most likely 'winning' already.

If you lost your way at some point in the short questionnaire, and that is going to apply to the majority of you I am sure, then you either just enjoy being a headless chicken and working 100 hours a week or you seriously want some help.

If the '100 hour per week chicken' profile is your key to happiness then again, you don't need this book. You can just carry on as you are and good luck to you. Contentment is a blessed thing and it is good that you have found yours.

But, if this has made you consider in any way that there might be some changes that you could make – if only you had some sort of guide and reference point – then you need to learn the art of productive laziness and, surprise, surprise, *The lazy winner* is a great place to start.

Try the questions again in the context of this book:

- Do I want to read *The lazy winner*? Do I need to read *The lazy winner*? Well you should have a clear view by now based on what you have read so far and on the answers to the questions above.
- Will the outcome of reading *The lazy winner* be worth the effort? Trust me, I will make it as painless as possible to get the most out of this book – working smarter not harder, I practice what I preach – you will gain in proportion to what you put into the process.
- Do I have to read *The lazy winner* myself? Ideally yes, but actually I can be hired at a ridiculous fee to come and read it to you – your choice, but why not give the book a go yourself first?
- If I have to read *The lazy winner* then what is the shortest path to the point of success? The book offers a flexible path to learning

---

4. You could invest in a 'get paid more/laid more' self-help book perhaps?

the art of productive laziness and I aim, as a smart but lazy author, to offer up multiple points of success along the way, chapter by chapter.

- What exactly is that point of success and at what stage will I just be wasting my time? When your chicken is no longer headless and you have reduced your working hours then you may well be reaching a point of return on your investment.

So, do you want to be a lazy winner or carry on being a busy loser?[5]

Hopefully I have demonstrated my integrity by being honest and upfront about what the book is and isn't. Out of that massive number of self-help books I noted earlier how many are actually read completely? How many are really used as they were intended? How many now sit on a shelf collecting dust or are destined for the next charity sale? We are all human, I know – we want to change but it is so hard sometimes and so much easier to just carry on with things as they are. I have twenty or so cookery books, beautifully produced with wonderful pictures and stimulating recipes, but I still, mostly, end up eating the same meals that I always have done. Strange.

OK, enough of me talking here, it time for you to make your mind up.

Decision time

So what is it going to be? You need to answer all of my questions but I know what you're thinking. 'Did he ask six questions or only five?'

Well, to tell you the truth, in all the excitement I kind of lost track myself, but being as this is a book about productive laziness,

---

5. OK so you are not a loser – what I meant by that phrase is that you could perhaps be losing out by not working in a more intelligent way.

the most powerful way of working in the world, and could blow your head clean off, you've got to ask yourself one question: Do I feel lucky? Well, do ya?

Go ahead reader, make my day...[6] Or to be more precise, go ahead and make your day by learning to work in a better way, the winning way of productive laziness.

Just remember:

'Progress isn't made by early risers. It's made by lazy men trying to find easier ways to do something.' [7]

---

6. 'Go ahead, make my day' is the catchphrase, written by Joseph C. Stinson and spoken by the character Harry Callahan, played by Clint Eastwood, in the 1983 film *Sudden Impact*. Note for Clint aficionados: the author has declined to address his audience as 'punk' in this instance. The previous quote (or misquote) is from the earlier *Dirty Harry*, a 1971 American crime thriller produced and directed by Don Siegel, the first in the Dirty Harry series.

7. From *Time Enough For Love*, Robert Heinlein, US science fiction author (1907–1988). Note: This is the quote that triggered the 'productively lazy' concept for me. Having trained many people over time in various jobs and roles I was constantly trying to explain how it was that I, and others, seemed to be so much more relaxed, organised, less stressed than others and yet delivered similar or better results. Reading Robert Heinlein's quote made it all seem so much clearer and simpler – I was 'lazy' and this was a good thing. A very good thing indeed I believe.

'Never be afraid to try something new.

Remember:

It was a lone amateur that built the Ark –
and a large group of professionals who built the Titanic.'

Dave Barry

Laziness

You are here

In order to help you navigate this book easily there will be regular tips to allow you to assess your progress on the path to productive laziness.[1] Think of it as a 'sat nav'[2] for productive laziness – it will guide you to your destination but won't get annoyed if you deviate in any way along the route or simply decide to go somewhere else if that seems a lot more interesting.

You are here

OK not particularly helpful at this point in time I know but we haven't really started yet have we? It will get more useful later on. But you are already not where you started: you have considered productive laziness and, presumably, decided that this is the path you wish to tread. So, you are already changing in a small but significant way.

---

1. It will also let you cheat if you want to – in a productively lazy way. After all, why should I (the self-proclaimed lazy master) expect you to read 30,000 words when I can make it easier and quicker for you?
2. 'Sat nav' is an abbreviation for the 'satellite navigation systems' designed for use in automobiles. They typically use a GPS (Global Positioning System) navigation device to acquire position data to locate the user on a road in the unit's map database. Using the road database, the unit can give directions to other locations along roads also in its database.

You just experienced productive laziness by the way.

As an added comfort to having parted with your hard-earned money (part of the reward for that 100-hour week being a headless chicken, perhaps), as if by magic, you have just experienced the productive laziness approach in the very decision making process that you went through.

By investing a small amount of time upfront you either just saved yourself the time and effort of reading another 29,000 words (plus a few pounds, dollars, yen, etc., depending on where you might have purchased this book), and gaining nothing from the experience, or you have prepared your mind to focus and learn to be generally more productive in the future. Both of these are good things.

Now we will begin in earnest.

Introducing Nigel

In which we meet the hero of our story, appreciate what it is that he feels about life and understand that he has a challenging and particular sense of humour – and keeps signs on his desk at work which present his insights about the world and where his mind is at right now.

This book could have been called *Making Plans for Nigel*.[3]

Nigel, our story's hero, is just this guy you know (for an alternative feel free to use Nigella).

---

3. If you would like to listen to Nigel(la)'s theme tune try 'Making plans for Nigel' by XTC. *Drums and Wires* is an XTC album released on 17 August 1979. It reached No. 34 on the UK album chart, and No. 176 on the US Billboard album charts. It contained the successful single 'Making Plans for Nigel', which was released on 14 September 1979, and reached No. 17 on the UK singles chart. Note: Using the masculine and feminine of Nigel has also allowed the author, in a moment of self-indulgence, to include the name of his favourite TV chef – Nigella Lawson – thereby winning a bet of some small financial but significant personal importance.

So this book could have been called *Making plans for Nigella*.

He (she) is pretty happy with his (her) life and could just keep on doing what he (she) has been doing for some time now but there is just a little something inside him (her) – OK I am going to stop this now. You get my meaning, I am trying to be completely sexually non-biased, therefore, from this point onwards can we take it as read that when I say him I also mean her and vice versa? Thank you.

Nigel is just like a lot of us. Life is what happens to Nigel while he was busy making other plans. Nigel likes a particular story about the meaning of life; he tells this one quite a lot.

On the first day God created the cow.

God said, 'You must go to the field with the farmer all day long and suffer under the sun, have calves and give milk to support the farmer. I will give you a life span of sixty years.' The cow said, 'That's kind of a tough life you want me to live for sixty years. Let me do it for twenty years and I'll give back the other forty.'

And God agreed.

On the second day God created the monkey.

God said, 'Entertain people, do monkey tricks, make them laugh. I'll give you a twenty year life span.' Monkey said, 'How boring, monkey tricks for twenty years? I don't think so. Cow gave you back forty, but I'll give back ten okay?'

Once again, God agreed.

On the third day, God created the dog.

God said, 'Sit all day by the door of your house and bark at anyone who comes in or walks past. I will give you a life span of twenty years.' The dog said, 'That's too long to be barking. Give me ten years and I'll give back the other ten.'

So God agreed.

On the fourth day God created man.

God said, 'Eat, sleep, play, have sex, enjoy. Do nothing, just enjoy life. I'll give you twenty years.' Man said, 'What? Only twenty years? No way. Tell you what: I'll take my twenty, and the forty cow gave back plus the ten monkey gave back, add that to the ten dog gave back and it makes eighty, okay?'

'Okay,' said God. 'You've got a deal.'

So that is why for the first twenty years we eat, sleep, play, have sex, enjoy, and do nothing; for the next forty years we slave in the sun to support our family; for the next ten years we do monkey tricks to entertain our grandchildren; and for the last ten years we sit in front of the house and bark at everybody!

Nigel isn't a bad man, despite the sense of humour, but he does feel that things could be somewhat better and in the back of his mind he senses that he could make some changes that would be good for him and for his family.

But what should he do? Why is he working so hard and for such long hours? Why is he so tired all of the time? And why does he never feel that he is up to date with anything or actually making some sort of progress? Why is his inbox and his 'to do' list so full? Life seems to be all about treading water. And why is that there are other people who seem to float around without a care in the world and yet achieve success in an effortless way? What is it that they do, or don't do, that Nigel doesn't, or does?

And why does he have a sign on his desk that reads 'Today is the tomorrow you worried about yesterday.'

What does 'winning' mean to you?

In which we understand what it means to be a 'winner' from a personal point of view, get scientific to a degree, and realise that there is an awful lot that we don't know we don't know – but all in a good way.

In order to track your progress you really need two points of reference. You need to know where you are now and you need to know where you would like to end up, eventually. It will be obvious to you, with perhaps some level of honest self-evaluation, where you are right now. But what about where you want to be, what does 'winning' mean to you in this context.

win (w n)
1. To achieve victory or finish first in a competition.
2. To achieve success in an effort or venture.

In this book I am not talking about the first definition, it is not about victory or coming first, and it isn't

'Winning is a personal journey. It's about reaching a destination you choose. At its most fundamental, winning is about achievement.'

Jack Welch[1]

---

1. John Francis 'Jack' Welch, Jr (born 19 November 1935) is an American chemical engineer, businessman and author. He was Chairman and CEO of General Electric between 1981 and 2001.

about others losing at your expense. It is all about the second definition, achieving your defined level of success in your work, your life, your effort.

So what is it that you would consider a 'win' in your life?

Warning, here comes the 'science' bit.

One way of looking at this is through the hierarchy of needs as laid out by Maslow.[2]

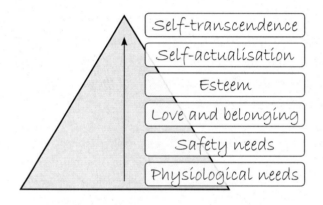

You can check out the appendix for more information about this but simply put, we are all motivated by our needs. Our most basic needs are inborn, having evolved over thousands of years. Abraham Maslow's Hierarchy of Needs helps to explain how these needs motivate us all.

---

2. Abraham Maslow's Hierarchy of Needs is a psychological theory proposed in his 1943 paper 'A Theory of Human Motivation'. Maslow subsequently extended the idea to include his observations of humans' innate curiosity. His theories parallel many other theories of human developmental psychology, all of which focus on describing the stages of growth in humans. Maslow studied what he called exemplary people such as Albert Einstein, Jane Addams, Eleanor Roosevelt and Frederick Douglass rather than mentally ill or neurotic people, writing that 'the study of crippled, stunted, immature, and unhealthy specimens can yield only a cripple psychology and a cripple philosophy.' Maslow studied the healthiest one per cent of the college student population and his theory was fully expressed in his 1954 book *Motivation and Personality.*

It states that we must satisfy each need in turn, starting with the first, which deals with the most obvious needs for survival itself: air, food, water and the ability to reproduce, clothing and shelter. Only when the lower order needs of physical and emotional well-being are satisfied are we concerned with the higher order needs of influence and personal development. Conversely, if the things that satisfy our lower order needs are swept away, we are no longer concerned about the maintenance of our higher order needs.

I am guessing that anyone reading this book is either not particularly focused on their current physiological needs or they have their priorities wildly out of balance.[3] Beyond that level of need if you ask most people what they want in life, and therefore, what they would like to move towards they will probably answer in the following terms:

- I would like peace of mind. Well, any definition of winning, and therefore success, will presumably have an element of this.
- I want to be healthy. Naturally, and any other form of success will pretty much be negated by a state of ill health.
- I want to be loved. This can be fulfilled by family or friends, a wife, a husband or a partner, through children or even animals.
- I want to be financially secure. This is often the freedom from thinking about money all of the time and not necessarily being 'rich'. Just having enough money to pay the bills, feed those in your care, and deal with basic necessities.
- I want to achieve something in life. We all desperately want to improve either ourselves, or someone, or something else. It is just human nature I guess.

---

3. If you are focused on your current physiological needs then perhaps you really should have invested in that 'get paid more/laid more' book instead of *The lazy winner*. Oh well, I am sure you can get a reasonable price for this book on eBay if you haven't bent the pages too much.

- I want to feel fulfilled. If you have dealt with the first five 'desires' but feel unfulfilled, then you aren't enjoying the full measure of your own success.

Defining your personal success can be done at two levels. You could go for the big 'where do I want to be in life in say five or ten years' time' approach and the 'what are my goals in life' approach. Answering those questions will give you a long-term plan for your personal destination of choice. Or you can answer at a lower level with the 'what things do I do that I could easily change that might make a real difference' and 'what is it that I do now that I know I shouldn't do' approach. This will at least point you in the right direction of the changes that would bring about a significant difference over time and an immediate difference quickly.

Personally I am always a fan of the 'quick win' approach. It delivers fast and it fuels the feeling of success and the momentum of achievement.[4]

We all want to succeed in more than just one area in our lives, so you do need to set multiple goals. For example, one goal may relate to your career and work while other goals may relate to your relationship, children, or hobbies. You need to ask yourself 'What kind of balance do I need in my life?' And you must find a balance between all these areas of your life in order for you to feel fulfilled.

Where are you?

So where are you now? What is your starting point for change?

The greater clarity you have in defining your 'journey' the more likely you are to succeed, or to put it another way – the less chance

---

4. It is here that *The lazy winner* will no doubt differ from the traditional self-help book that often demands big changes for a big reward. I am with Confucius when he said 'A journey of a thousand miles begins with a single step.' And I like to make those first steps very small ones if I can.

you have of getting lost on the way. The other great benefit of seeing the full journey is that you can plot your simple steps and not be put off by a belief that any change is just way too enormous and far too difficult to achieve (so why bother trying).

The easiest thing to do is to start with what you know.

• Do you know what you want?
• Do you know what you don't want?

For example you might think 'I want to spend more time with my family but I don't want to do a bad job at work and not have a career'. This is perfectly acceptable and aligns itself to the guidance of having balance in what you do.

It is possible that you don't know what you want, or even worse, you don't know what you don't want.

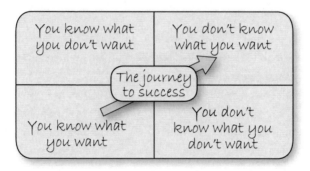

The journey to success can only be plotted once you have a clear route mapped out.

Part of this, in the interest of not wasting time and effort, is in avoiding the things that you don't want and focusing on the things that you do want. It is a little like going for a walk. There are two types of walk: the 'A' to 'B' type where the purpose is to get to 'B' from a starting point of 'A'. And there is the second type where you have plenty of time and the pleasure in the walk is to take your time and discover interesting places on the way. For a 'productive but lazy' person the 'A' to 'B' journey is the one to go for – in fact a truly 'productively lazy' approach would look at whether you could in fact miss 'B' out altogether and go straight to 'C', if 'C' is your next destination.

Let's start with your journey now.

Can you now list everything that you believe you do want and would like to change? Honesty is really important here – just put it down on paper or electronically, your choice, but put it down somewhere.

What about the things that you know you don't want? Can you list these as well?

Take some time now to do this.

1. What do you want?
2. What don't you want?

Yes, I know that first list is going to be a whole lot easier to put together than the second one, but the more you understand about yourself and what you want the better.

Great, now we move on to the other part of the journey.

Now, can you think about how you would find out about the things that you might well want if only you knew what they were? Talking to other people often helps here – widening your scope of knowledge and experience through others (we will look at your network of influence later on).

What about the things that you don't know that you don't want? Well perhaps all you can do here is anticipate that, as you progress along your path to change, you will probably stray into this area once or twice so be ready. If it doesn't feel right then challenge it.

This is not a one-time only self assessment – you will need to re-test yourself with the questions of need and desire several times over as your journey progresses.

'Efficiency is intelligent laziness.'

David Dunham

Do you want this and do you need this? Remember these key questions and that it is the combination of answers to them that should inform you of your final decision, not one of them alone. Just because you want to do something doesn't mean you should do it.

This is not a 'one time' assessment

Keep checking back to make sure you are progressing in the right direction.

Nigel has a plan

Nigel was wandering through the shops near his office during a rare lunch break. Pretty much everyone he needed to talk to or who needed to talk to him was otherwise occupied and so he took advantage of the lull by actually going out of the building for something to eat. And now he was heading back along the 'scenic' route through the shops. His eye caught a book promotion in the window of the book store – *The lazy winner: How to do more with less effort and succeed in your work and personal life without rushing around like a headless chicken or putting in 100-hour weeks.* Intriguing, maybe he needed some of that.

Nigel had his fair share of shelf-fill (as he called those many books that filled his bookshelves but that he had never actually read all the way through, and even in some cases, never started). He thought that if someone could come up with a book that incorporated the seven ways of this and the nine ideals of that with a hint of who moved my one day working week, dusted off with a topping of just eat that gerbil then they would clean up. In a big way.

It reminded Nigel of a joke.

A man goes in to the local bookstore and asks the assistant for the self-help section. The assistant replied 'If I tell you that then you will gain nothing from the experience of finding it yourself.'

But Nigel lingered and stared at the book. He sure needed some help so why not splash out a small amount and give it a go. If the worst came to the worst he was pretty sure there was a small gap on the bookshelf that was still exposing some wood.

At home that evening Nigel sat down and opened the pages of his new purchase. The euphoria of buying and then owning the book had worn off long ago – that heady moment when he actually felt more productive just by owning the creation – but he had spent the money so why not check it out.

To be fair it wasn't just a rash purchase as he had read the first chapter which had openly given him the opportunity to put the book back down and walk out of the store without handing any money over to the assistant. In fact it had actively encouraged him to think about buying a completely different book that promised to improve his sex life, among other benefits.

But he hadn't been tempted. He was now the proud owner of *The lazy winner*, or at least he was the owner of *The lazy winner*.

He took a sip of his coffee, opened the book, and began to read …

What exactly is productive laziness?

In which, with the aid of an Italian economist, we learn that not everything is as important as everything else but rather, some things are really important, and focus and planning is what it is all about.

We all know about the 80/20 rule, let's start there.

The Pareto Principle (also known as the 80/20 rule) states that for many phenomena 80% of consequences stem from 20% of the causes. It's commonly misused, for example, it is a misuse to state that a solution to a problem 'fits the 80/20 rule' just because it fits 80% of the cases; it must be implied that this solution requires only 20% of the resources needed to solve all cases.

The principle was in fact suggested by management thinker Joseph M. Juran and it was named after the Italian economist Vilfredo Pareto,[1] who observed that 80% of property in Italy was owned by 20% of the Italian population. The assumption is that most of the results in any situation are determined by a small number of causes.

---

1. Vilfredo Federico Damaso Pareto (1848–1923) was an Italian engineer, sociologist, economist, and philosopher. He made several important contributions to economics, particularly in the study of income distribution and in the analysis of individuals' choices. His legacy as an economist was profound. Partly because of him, the field evolved from a branch of moral philosophy as practiced by Adam Smith into a data intensive field of scientific research and mathematical equations.

So, '20% of clients may be responsible for 80% of sales volume'. This can be evaluated and is likely to be roughly right, and can be helpful in future decision making. The Pareto Principle also applies to a variety of more mundane matters: one might guess that we wear approximately 20% of our most favoured clothes about 80% of the time;[2] perhaps we spend 80% of the time with 20% of our acquaintances and so on.

The Pareto Principle or 80/20 rule can and should be used by every smart but lazy person in their daily life. The value of the Pareto Principle for you is that it reminds you to focus on the 20% that matters.

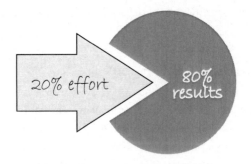

Woody Allen once said '80% of success is showing up.' I'm not so sure about that. No, better to appreciate that of the things you do during your day only 20% really matter. That 20% produces 80% of the results.

Only 20% of what you do really matters – so focus on that!

So, you should begin by both identifying and focusing on that 20% and drop the other 80% for now.

---

2. For some strange reason my wife, Lisa, insists that we spend huge amounts of time at the weekends shopping for the 80% of her clothes, shoes and handbags that she rarely wears. I have explained the Pareto Principle to her on numerous occasions but to avail. We still shop a lot!

What was it that you achieved yesterday that made you feel good – made you feel that your efforts were most rewarded – that progressed something at work that was important – or dealt with something in your personal life that needed doing.

Consider yesterday. I bet that you will be able to identify one, two, or maybe even three things that you did that gave you the most return on your personal investment.

Each day it is important to give yourself some time to think calmly about what it is that you should do; whether that is in the car, on the bus, or on the train, or perhaps in your office, at your desk enjoying that first coffee of the day. It can even be the night before. It is entirely up to you, just pick a time that will allow you to think about the day's tasks and prioritise what you want to achieve. What is important – what is the 20% that will deliver the 80%?

The devil is in the 'to do' list.

It is easy to build up a wonderful 'to do' list and even to cross some things off the list as well. But that is not necessarily progress.

To do:
Nothing

You arrive in the office and you have a 'to do' list already in place: get coffee, sharpen pencil, book haircut, pick up lettuce from the supermarket, and so on. And what happens? Well the list gets added to rapidly as you meet people at work and the phone goes and you get invited to meetings and the email starts to flood in. But just numbering the list from one to one hundred means nothing, this is just a time stamped list or a list of when you thought of the

'All of the biggest technological inventions created by man – the airplane, the automobile, the computer – say little about his intelligence, but speak volumes about his laziness.'

Mark Kennedy

things that you needed to do. You need to prioritise the list. Validate the return on your investment against each one. Ask the questions of need and desire.[3] Do you need to do this? Do you want to do this? And then consider the importance of doing each one.

You could easily complete and cross off 50% of that list and still not have really made any progress. You could, in fact, cross off 80% of that list having achieved only 20% of your expected outcomes if you skilfully avoid the 20% of the tasks that are most important.

So you need to weigh each task and identify its importance. Once you have done that then you can get on with the job of doing the things on the list.

Now I am not saying not to do the complete list in the end, I am just saying that there is enormous value in thinking, planning, prioritising and then focusing. In fact get the 'big ones' out of the way and you will feel so good that the others will simply get done with the minimum of apparent

Think – Plan – Prioritise – Focus

effort. Another way of looking at it is that eliminating the 80% of the work that only gets 20% of your results potentially enables you to invest the 80% on something else – I am not entirely sure that this will work but maybe the answer lies somewhere between the two approaches?

If you are interested (and maybe want to confuse your boss if they ask you what you are up to), Pareto madness[4] can be achieved in the following way:

---

3. OK I am coming clean here, much as it pains me to do so. A small (almost invisible) 'thank you' should be noted at this point to someone who might be called Nick and who probably won't read this book anyway as unless I give him a copy he won't pay for one. Why? He always sets the tests of 'Do I want it?' and 'Do I need it?' This book will probably fail both tests. It struck me that, while I have always thought this way to some extent, the repetitious 'need' and 'desire' combination does clarify an element of 'productive laziness'.

4. You can, perhaps, get even more efficient – if the parameters in the Pareto distribution are suitably chosen, then one would have not only 80% of effects coming from 20% of causes, but also 80% of that top 80% of effects coming from 20% of that top 20% of causes, and so on (80% of 80% is 64%; 20% of 20% is 4%, so this implies a '64/4 law').

- Take five people;
- Remove the 80% of their work that results in only 20% of their results;
- Combine the five lots of the 20% of their activity that results in 80% of their results and you now have one job for one person resulting in five times the results.

Think about it but don't try it at home (or work)!

All of this is the first step to becoming even more effective by avoiding working long hours on tasks that don't need to be worked on while doing a more productive job on those that do matter.

Less is definitely more if you want to be productively lazy.

The whole 'more haste, less speed' principle applies here as well. When we are Less = More in a hurry, we often end up completing a task more slowly, making mistakes on the way, having to rework or recover effort, and – like the tortoise and the hare – the calmer, steady approach often wins out.[5]

A lot to remember I know but we are back to giving yourself time to think things through and decide the best way forward whenever possible. And when you do that you can consider the aspects of simplification, scalability and reusability.

Effort now will save effort later on.

---

5. One of Aesop's Fables that is actually a moral story about overconfidence but is often reflected on as a message about taking a calm and steady approach to something, as the winner of the race, the tortoise, declares, 'Slowly does it every time!'

Nigel thinks about laziness

Nigel now has a list of things he would like to change. It isn't a long list as he decided to keep it as simple as possible and to leave some room to add in some things that he might discover later on.

He just wants to have a little more time to prepare for things and to plan things and not always be rushed.

He would like to escape the office just a little earlier than he does now.

There is a poster on the wall in the coffee room at Nigel's work that reads:

'So you want a day off. Let's take a look at what you are asking for:

- There are 365 days per year available for work.
- There are 52 weeks per year in which you already have 2 days off per week, leaving 261 days available for work.
- Since you spend 16 hours each day away from work, you have used up 170 days, leaving only 91 days available.
- You spend 30 minutes each day on coffee breaks which accounts for 23 days each year, leaving only 68 days available.
- With a 1 hour lunch each day, you have used up another 46 days, leaving only 22 days available for work.
- You normally spend 2 days per year on sick leave. This leaves you only 20 days per year available for work.
- We have 5 public holidays per year, so your available working time is down to 15 days.
- The company generously gives 14 days holiday per year which leaves only 1 day available for work and the company would appreciate it if you worked hard on this day.
- So 'no' you can't have time off!

Nigel feels that the one day he apparently works according to this poster seems to go on for an awfully long time. Nigel doesn't think he is a lazy man, and in fact he knows a joke about this.

A man told his doctor that he wasn't able to do all the things around the house that he used to do. The doctor started a long and thorough examination, but finally found nothing wrong with the man.

When the examination was complete, he said, 'Now, Doc, I can take it. Tell me in plain English what is wrong with me.'

The doctor replied, 'Well, in plain English, you are just lazy.'

'Okay,' said the man. 'Now give me the medical term so I can tell my wife.'

Nigel would like a little more 'me' time without losing any 'family' time on the way and he knows that neither his wife nor his family think that he is at all lazy in that way.

The idea of productive laziness appeals to Nigel. Having read this section of the book, it seems to make sense and there also seem to be some strong supporters of the idea out there. He was well aware of the 80/20 rule, he used it himself in describing his company's customers, 20% of whom deliver 80% of the revenue, but he had never thought of applying it to himself in any way before.

The 'Think – Plan – Prioritise – Focus' approach is just logical when he considers it and Nigel freely admits that he has one of the longest 'to do' lists that you can imagine. In fact, if he is honest, he has a 'to do' list of 'to do' lists covering home, work, his personal life (way down the bottom of the pile) and 'stuff'.

In Nigel's mind there is no progress being made right now and he is neither a wise nor a lazy man.

Things need to change.

Success

The strength of 'No'

In which it is explained that there are many ways to say no and how important it is to use some of those ways perhaps a little more than we have done so far in order to fulfil the need and the desire tests.

Making a productively lazy list is all well and good but one of the real consequences of doing this and changing the way that you are going to work in the future, will be the need for (and of course the benefit of) saying 'no' a whole lot more often.

Most of us know that we really should say 'no' a little more often than we do, but for some reason it is difficult to utter the necessary noise that would deliver this decision.

And yet, in contrast, my kids seem to have absolutely no problem with saying it many times each day.[1] When we are tiny it seems the only word we can utter is 'no' as we try to assert ourselves in the big wide world. But as we get older we tend to feel guilty when we have to say 'no' to other people. We regularly give in because we just can't stand the thought of upsetting others, being seen as 'mean', or just don't want to make a fuss.

There is another factor I believe. If you say 'yes' then the conversation is pretty much over. The other person might start to explain in detail what you need to do to complete the thing that you have just agreed to do but for you, the apparent effort is over. Now on the other hand, saying 'no' will most likely require you

---

1. I did ask them if I could use their names in this book but they all said a definite 'no' – that is typical of Jenny, Adam, Sam and Scott!

to immediately put in some additional effort in justifying why you have said 'no' and why you can't, don't want to, shouldn't do it, etc. A 'yes' equates to less effort now (but a whole lot more later), while a 'no' equates to effort right now, up front, immediately (but conversely a lot less later on).

But saying 'no' can actually be a good thing for all involved and can definitely be a good thing for you.

Well it's not '50 ways to leave your lover'[2] but more 'fifty ways to leave something alone that you are better off not getting involved in'. To aid your capability in responding in the negative here are some helpful words:

1. *Nie* – Afrikaans
2. *Jo* – Albanian
3. *La* – Arabic
4. *Nie* – Belarusian
5. *Na* – Bengali
6. *Ne* – Bulgarian
7. *No* – Catalan
8. *Bù* – Chinese
9. *Non* – Creole (Haiti)
10. *No* – Croatian
11. *Ne* – Czech
12. *Ikke* – Danish
13. *Geen* – Dutch
14. *No* – English
15. *Ei* – Estonian
16. *Ei* – Finnish

---

2. '50 Ways to Leave Your Lover' was a 1975 hit song by Paul Simon, from his album *Still Crazy After All These Years*. '50 Ways to Leave Your Lover' broke in the US in late December 1975 becoming No. 1 in the US Billboard Hot 100 on 7 February 1976 and remaining there for three weeks. It was certified gold on 11 March 1976, and remained a best-seller for nearly five months. The song also topped the adult contemporary chart for two weeks. It remains Simon's biggest solo hit. On the UK Singles Chart, the song reached No. 23 in January 1976.

17. *Non* – French
18. *Ara* – Georgian
19. *Nein* – German
20. *Ókhi* – Greek
21. *Lo* – Hebrew (Israel)
22. *Nahi* – Hindi
23. *Nem* – Hungarian
24. *Nei* – Icelandic
25. *Tidak* – Indonesian
26. *No* – Italian
27. *Wa* – Japanese
28. *Aniyo* – Korean
29. *Ne* – Latvian
30. *Néra* – Lithuanian
31. *Ne* – Macedonian
32. *Tidak* – Malay
33. *Ma* – Maltese
34. *Ikke* – Norwegian
35. *Na* - Persian (Farsi)
36. *Nie* – Polish
37. *Não* – Portuguese
38. *Nu* – Romanian
39. *Niet* – Russian
40. *Nema* – Serbian
41. *Ne* – Slovak
42. *Brez* – Slovenian
43. *No* – Spanish
44. *Hakuna* – Swahili
45. *Ingen* – Swedish
46. *Mïmi* – Thai
47. *Yok* – Turkish
48. *Nei* – Ukrainian
49. *Không* – Vietnamese
50. *Nid oes* – Welsh

'Learn to say "no" to
the good so you can say
"yes" to the best.'

John C. Maxwell

Now here is something interesting. Out of all those languages the longest word for 'no' is six letters, the shortest is two letters, and the average is three letters. So again, why is it such a difficult word to say? I mean there are much tougher words to enunciate – such as 'pneumonoultramicroscopicsilicovolcanoconiosis'.[3]

When someone asks you to do something you really don't want to do you need to learn to say 'no' – simply 'no'. You don't have to avoid replying, apologise or make up excuses, in fact making up excuses tends only to make matters worse over time. You just need to say it clearly and firmly. After all, it is your choice.

In many cases, not saying 'no' becomes one of the greatest challenges to our own productivity. What happens in these situations is that we place the satisfaction of others ahead of our own.

Why on earth do we do this when most likely we do know better? Well there are many different reasons:

- We want to help other people. Some supposedly positive behaviours are confused with other supposedly negative behaviours. Refusing to do something is considered to be a selfish act, while accepting something is seen as a non-selfish act, both altruistic and generous.
- We fear rejection by other people. We all want to be liked by others, therefore we seek their approval, often at a cost to ourselves.
- We fear losing potential opportunities from other people. We believe that if we say 'no' now then in the future we won't be offered other interesting opportunities.

---

3. An obscure term ostensibly referring to a lung disease caused by silica dust, sometimes cited as one of the longest words in the English language (45 letters in total). If you find that one easy try 'Llanfairpwllgwyngyllgogerychwyrn-drobwllllantysiliogogogoch', which is a large village and community on the island of Anglesey in Wales, situated on the Menai Strait next to the Britannia Bridge and across the strait from Bangor. The village is best known for its name, the longest place name in Europe, and one of the longest place names in the world. Either way you have to admit 'no' is a lot simpler.

- We respect other people. Sometimes we feel that another person just doesn't deserve a 'no' response from us.
- We experience guilt when we don't help other people. We are often quite worried after saying ' no', even if it is the right and proper thing to do. Human nature leads us to feel concerned.

And perhaps the most common one:

- We are fearful of confrontation with other people. We want to avoid unnecessary conflict and maintain a good and happy atmosphere.

All of these are indeed reasons that we find saying 'no' difficult but none of them are good reasons to not say 'no'. Try to resolve to say 'no' more often. It won't hurt you – honestly – and it won't hurt other people either if you are sensible and sensitive.

Prioritise your valuable time and don't be persuaded to waste it just to please someone else.

It doesn't mean you are being selfish, but sometimes you do need to put your own needs first.

You might say 'no' for a good

Ask yourself the important questions:

Do I want to do this piece of work, job or task? Even I do want to do it, do I need to do it?

Is the result or outcome worth my effort?

reason other than the fact that you don't want to do it, or need to do it. You might, for example, say 'no' because there is a much better qualified person who could do the job in a far more effective way in a shorter time than you could.

The principle here is that allocating work to the best-suited person benefits everyone in the long run. Of course this cannot be done just to avoid work. You have to pick up some actions yourself

Ask yourself the important question:

Do I have to do it myself?

otherwise you will never achieve anything. And there is the 'what goes around comes around' idea as well. Sometimes you shouldn't say 'no' because despite the fact that you may not want to do something, need to do something and there is someone who could do it better, you do want to help out and be that team player or Good Samaritan. Or, it is in your interests to take on a project so you can learn some new skills, in which case you may well not be the most obvious person for the job.

It is all about balance and priority. Overall you want to deal with the important stuff plus a reasonable amount of other stuff.

If you keep saying 'yes' then your backlog will never go down and you will spend far too much time working on the unimportant.

The skill of 'Yes'

In which we appreciate that the right yes is so important and that even this yes should be adapted to your personal commitments in order to offer the greatest chance of overall success.

What happens when you do say 'yes'?

We have had the 'fifty ways to say no' so why not 'five ways to say yes' (well I do want to encourage you to say 'no' more often than you say 'yes').

1. If I have to.
2. OK.
3. Good.
4. Great.
5. What are we waiting for?

'If I have to' isn't such a great way to get on board and won't win you many friends or influence people. It smacks of an attitude and a reluctance that shouldn't be there. If you have done all of your pre-work and considered all of the relevant questions – need, desire, appropriate person, duty – then you are going to do it, so why not do it with a smile and with enthusiasm. It may well turn out to be one of the 'I don't know what I do want' situations and you might have fun. Either way if you do the task well and happily then 'what goes around comes around' may well benefit you later on in life.

'OK' is, well, OK. You are on board and will no doubt do the best that you can.

'Good' takes a step up the ladder of enthusiasm and a 'great' sounds like you will put everything you have into the business of successfully completing the work to the best of your ability.

Best of all is 'What are we waiting for' as this shows that not only will you put 100% effort behind this and do a super job, you will most likely take the lead as you clearly feel strongly both that this needs to be done and done by you.

Available to promise – a qualified 'yes'

But 'yes' can be less 'black and white', it can also be a subtle shade of grey. In a very good way.

This is the concept of 'ATP' which stands for 'available to promise'.[1] It is used a lot in manufacturing and sales but simply put it means that you can say 'yes' but then qualify that with a consideration of what it is that you can promise someone now, tomorrow, next week or next month. If the work needs doing and you are signed up for it (somewhere between a 'if I have to' and a 'what are we waiting for') then can you do more if you wait a while? Can you do even more if you wait a little while longer?

> 'A 'No' uttered from the deepest conviction is better than a 'Yes' merely uttered to please, or worse, to avoid trouble.'
>
> Mahatma Gandhi

When you agree to do something think carefully about the real urgency and the potential benefit of holding back for a while. You might do a much better piece of work if you didn't rush in right now and that might be beneficial to everyone rather than an 'OK'

---

1. Available to promise (ATP) is a business function that provides a response to customer order enquiries, based on resource availability. It generates available quantities of the requested product, and delivery due dates. Items can be promised to customer order requirements for a given period based on an uncommitted or available status, calculated as: on-hand inventory, less booked customer orders, plus expected master schedule receipts for the period.

delivery now. Talk to the recipient of your planned efforts and explain that they could say, have a little now, a little more fairly quickly, but if they want the whole then they would have to wait a bit longer.

Say 'no' firmly – say 'yes' when a 'yes' is appropriate – say 'how much and how soon' openly – and be clear in all that you say and do.

Beware the double positive

A linguistics professor was lecturing to her class one day.

'In English,' she said, 'A double negative forms a positive.[2] In some languages, though, such as Russian, a double negative is still a negative. However, there is no language wherein a double positive can form a negative.'

A voice from the back of the room piped up, 'Yeah, right.'

---

2. A double negative occurs when two forms of negation are used in the same clause. In most logics and some languages, double negatives cancel one another and produce an affirmative. In other languages, doubled negatives intensify the negation. The rhetorical term for this effect, when it leads to an understated affirmation, is litotes. Triple negation, quadruple negation, and so on can also be seen, which leads to the terms multiple negation or negative concord.

Nigel learns when to say yes and when to say no

Nigel had just put the phone down and stood looking blankly out into the middle distance for a moment or two. What had happened? He knew the call was coming and he knew what he was going to be asked and he had absolutely, without a shadow of a doubt, 100% definite, decided that he would kindly, politely, but firmly say 'no'.

'What did you say then?'

'I said yes,' sighed Nigel

But why had he said yes when less than 0.000001% of him wanted to say yes – all the rest of him wanted to scream 'no' at the top of his voice.

'Why did you do that?' came the query.

'Because...' came Nigel's wilting reply.

Yes, just because. Because he had done what he always did in such situations, he played the nice person role and agreed to help. But now he had two problems. The first was that he actually had more than enough work right now and precious little time to spare, well no spare time if truth be told. And secondly he had just broken the 'productive lazy' rule he was trying to follow. Not a good start.

He had spent some quiet time only the evening before and thought about what he wanted. He had completed the journey planner for the things that he knew he wanted to do and that he wanted to change, and he had attempted to write down some of the things he knew that he didn't want. The components of unknown things he left for later – even the list that he had put together had taken some time and more than one cup of coffee.

He also realised that to achieve any change he needed to address his 'yes man' style of conversation and then the phone had rung today and what did he do? He said 'no' in his head but a big cheery 'yes' came out of his mouth and down the telephone line.

So 'yes' it had been.

A joke wandered into his mind.

A man's wife asked him if a certain dress made her bum[3] look big. He answered, 'Not as much as the dress that you wore yesterday.'

Of course, the correct response for all sensible married men would have been, 'Certainly not, you are looking very attractive and anyway, you don't have a large bum.'

Nigel realised that with the right incentive, even he could say 'no' at the appropriate moment.

He looked back at the book and discounted using any of the fifty ways to say 'no' and skipped the 'saying yes' section as he had already done that, but he did reread the 'available to promise' section and then made his mind up. He had a cunning plan.

'I have a cunning plan,' announced Nigel as he reached once more for the telephone.

A phone call later and Nigel declared, 'That's better.'

'What is?'

'I have confirmed that I can help out but that with my other commitments I would have to hold off for two weeks or so,' smiled Nigel.

'Good for you.'

'Yes' laughed Nigel 'ATP! The deployment of my cunning plan.'

Nigel is thinking of replacing the sign on his desk with one saying 'Mean what you say and say what you mean – it's a whole lot quicker that way'.

---

3. In the interests of global sales 'bum', a very nice English word, can be taken to mean ass, a very nice American word, or arse, a less nice English word and indeed butt, a less nice and overly used (by my kids at least) American word. Your choice.

'Change always comes
bearing gifts.'

Price Pritchett

How can being 'lazy' make you more successful?

In which we assess precisely why doing less can actually let you succeed more, with the right attitude naturally, and uncover the really important things that you should be doing.

There are a number of questions that you should ask yourself:

- Do I want to do this piece of work, job or task? Even if I do want to do it, do I need to do it?
- Is the result or outcome worth my effort?
- Do I have to do it myself?
- If I have to do it then what is the shortest path to the point of success?
- What exactly is that point of success and at what stage will I just be wasting my time?

What we will do now is work our way through these questions and challenge, at each step, your current thinking and behaviour.

Want and need

We have seen that the reason you should be doing this is that your efforts should be focused on the 20% that matters, at least to begin with, and the only way you can do this is to assess each task or job as it is placed in front of you. Your 'to do' list needs to be sharp, focused and definitely relevant to what you are trying to achieve.

The starting point should be the 'do I want to' and the 'do I need to' questions. Always ask them together in order to come up with the right answer.

Is there a compelling reason for doing a task or not? If not then don't do it.

If the answer formulates as a 'yes' then it may be time to move ahead.

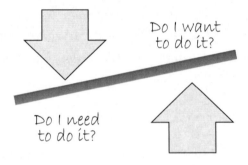

Worthy of effort

The second stage after the 'want' and 'need' evaluation is the consideration of whether the outcome expected is worth the anticipated effort.

These elements evaluate the 20% and we then consider the likely outcome.

A better person

With three 'yeses' in the bag it is still not a done deal just yet. Consider now whether, even though you want to do something, you really are the right person to actually carry out the task. Is there someone better qualified who can and will do a better and perhaps faster job than you?

If there is why are you thinking about doing it?

The important stuff

Having allowed yourself some time to think about what it is that you should focus on and therefore also allowed yourself the benefit of doing some simple planning, you can focus on the important stuff, as opposed to worrying about the less important stuff.

You have asked the first three important questions and now the buck really does rest with you because you are committed, you are taking ownership of this one.

But even now the 'less is more' mantra should be sounding in your mind.

When you do get on to doing the things that you should do then consider this:

- Can you automate it? Can you scale it? Can you make it reusable in a wider context? Use that creativity that you have, that all productively lazy people have, and make 'it' repeatable, suitable for a wider purpose and audience, easily available without you having to act as a gatekeeper all the time (thereby taking up your time).
- Can you simplify it? Can you shorten it? If there's something that you do that is complicated and difficult, find ways to make it easier and simpler. List the steps, and see which can be eliminated or streamlined. Which steps can be done by someone else or automated or dropped completely? What is absolutely the easiest way to do this?
- Can it wait? Is it really needed when it is supposed to be needed? Will it impact on others if it waits? Sometimes, not always you understand, but just sometimes, not rushing into something can turn out to be a productively good thing as it turns out it didn't matter anyway, or at least the need

Scale it – make it reusable

Simplify it – shorten it

Wait until it is really needed – is it needed?

has gone away. We live in a complex butterfly and hurricane world[1] of interaction so at any given time just about everything is changing.

At every opportunity you must think your actions through to the end, as best that you can, and aim to optimize your personal return on your personal investment.

Clinical

If all of this sounds rather cold and clinical, even cynical in some cases, it really isn't. It should be second nature to all of us to consider each request, to promise only what we can realistically deliver, and to be honest with ourselves about what we want in life.

---

1. 'When a butterfly flutters its wings in one part of the world, it can eventually cause a hurricane in another' Edward Lorenz, pioneer of Chaos Theory. 'Butterflies and Hurricanes' is also a song by Muse from their third album, *Absolution*, and was the last single released from the album. It was one of two songs recorded with a string section, both of which were recorded, along with an early version of 'Apocalypse Please', during the initial stages of recording. The song is notable for its Rachmaninoff-esque piano interlude. The song concerns itself with the so-called butterfly effect of Chaos Theory, describing how even tiny changes in present conditions, like the flap of a butterfly's wing, can cause big differences in the future.

Nigel just gets on with it

Nigel was feeling quite pleased with himself. Not only had he managed to adapt his original 'yes' to the most recent request for help, he later got a phone call that relieved him of all responsibilities.

'It turned out that it really needed doing a bit sooner than I could manage and there is someone else who would be pretty good at the job, probably better than me actually, so they asked her instead,' explained Nigel to a work colleague over a morning coffee.

Later on Nigel's mind went back to the chapter in the book he had read last night, about the 'less is more' mantra and it struck him that this was all good common sense.

He also reflected on the 'to do' list that he had now and immediately highlighted in his mind the one task he knew he had been putting off for some time now.

'Time to face the worst,' declared Nigel to anyone in hearing distance, and he cleared his mind and his desk ready to tackle the 'big one'.

Nigel really didn't fancy having to buy a sign for his desk that said 'Why do today what you can put off until tomorrow'. That didn't seem to be in the spirit of productive laziness at all.

All he needed was the right incentive to just get on with it. A joke floated into his mind at this point.

A lorry driver, who had never owned a mobile phone, was a frequent user of the pay telephone at a certain roadside café. He was greatly inconvenienced when the phone broke down one day.

He made repeated requests for it to be repaired but sadly the telephone company only made promises and never actually arrived to fix the issue.

After several days he decided to contact the phone company again and told them that there was no longer any hurry to repair the phone. He added that the phone was now working fine, 'except that the money is being returned to callers upon completion of each call'.

A repairman arrived within the hour.

Having cleared his mind of any doubts that he was going to finally crack this one, this time, Nigel explored the challenge from every angle he could think of. He made calls to validate the current status, he made calls to gather more insight and understanding, he made calls to seek help and advice, and then he decided on a plan of action.

He actually felt better for just getting on with it. It was as if the 'problem' became perceptibly bigger, more complex, uglier, through the very process of ignoring it. When it was brought out into the light and the open maybe it wasn't quite as big as Nigel had thought it was.

Either way, Nigel was on the road to getting the damn thing off his 'to do' list once and for all.

Opportunity

'Luck is what happens when preparation meets opportunity.'

Seneca

Flexibility meets opportunity

In which we appreciate that in order to leave ourselves open and ready for new opportunities, or to address urgent matters that suddenly arise, we cannot operate at 100% all of the time.

Think about this: every time you reduce your 'work in progress' (WIP) limit, the amount or percentage of your time that is committed at any given moment to tasks and jobs underway, then you are automatically improving your flexibility for addressing new activities without impacting on this WIP. You are effectively increasing your 'not work in progress' (NWIP), the amount or percentage of your time that is not committed at any given moment.

If you don't take this approach and you 'run to the max' all of the time you will naturally:

- Burn yourself out at some point.
- Hit times when you have more to do than you can physically (and mentally) handle.

Many of us can be hugely effective when under extreme pressure, and that is great, but it is not a sustainable model – something will give eventually and it is most likely to be you.

Flexible working is a key way of achieving real success, in not disappointing anyone you have commitments with, but in being open and ready as and when new 'work' appears on the immediate horizon.

For all you know in the next twenty-four hours that 'opportunity' that you had longed for might just turn up in the post, through a meeting, as part of a phone call, and how will you feel if you have to decline the chance to get on board, join in or take ownership all because you were just too committed already?

Don't miss out on opportunities because you were too busy!

Or perhaps something that you didn't anticipate happens that demands your immediate attention and, as a result, you have to drop something else that you really wanted (and needed) to do?

In both cases you will be disappointed but it will be because you planned it this way. You didn't allow yourself the flexibility to be versatile – 100% is not a good thing.

Try this quick exercise to check your 'versatility' factor.

1. Think about your next working day – how many hours in the day will you be active, that is not sleeping? This is your finite capacity (unless you are capable of time travel) for 'doing stuff'.
2. OK, now list all of the things that you have to do. Include everything: eating, washing, travelling, emails, meetings, phone calls, personal activities, social communication, etc.
3. Now allocate time in hours or parts of hours against each task – it is important here that you be very, very honest with yourself. Don't kid yourself that you only spend ten minutes emailing each day, or that you can get to the office in under twenty-five minutes.
4. Right, now you can add it all up… actually before you do that just go back over the estimates of time once more for me and give yourself a last chance to be really, truly, completely and utterly honest with yourself. Change the numbers if your conscience tells you to do so and then add it all up again…

So what did you end up with? How many hours out of your finite capacity limit have you committed?

What percentage is left free to deal with the unplanned and unexpected?

If it is less than 20%[1] then I feel that you are kidding yourself a little and would recommend that you look again at what is on that list and what you could perhaps not do, do less of, get help with and so on.

We spoke earlier about a journey. 'It is a little like going for a walk, there are two types of walk: the 'A' to 'B' type where the purpose is to get to 'B' from a starting point of 'A'. And there is the second type where you have plenty of time and the pleasure in the walk is to take your time and discover interesting places on the way. For a 'productive but lazy' person the 'A' to 'B' journey is the one to go for – in fact in a truly 'productively lazy' approach you would see if you could in fact miss out 'B' altogether and go straight to 'C', if 'C' was your next destination. Well, by allowing yourself the right degree of flexibility, occasionally, you can opt to take the slower, more scenic journey and find some new and interesting sights.

> Remember:
> Think – Plan –
> Prioritise – Focus

Take the time now to consider the list that you have made and, as a start, aim to reduce or eliminate at least one of the items on that list – and hey, that shouldn't be 'eating' or 'breathing'!

---

1. Hey look at that, we are back with the good old 80/20 rule once more. Incidentally the Pareto Principle was a prominent part of the 2007 bestseller *The 4-Hour Workweek* by Tim Ferriss in which the author recommended focusing one's attention on that 20% that contributes 80% of your income. More notably, he also recommends firing those 20% of customers who take up the majority of one's time and cause the most trouble. In terms of your personal priorities you might want to think about 'firing' the 20% of activities that are least important so that you can do a better job on the 80% that do matter and be flexible for new opportunities.

There is a glass of water on the table...

One man might say, 'It's half-full.' He is traditionally considered an optimist.

A second man might say, 'It's half-empty.' He is traditionally considered a pessimist.

A third man might say 'It's twice as big as it needs to be.' He is probably a management consultant and will give you a bill to back up his analysis.[2]

But the productively lazy person should say: 'The glass is fine and the drink is fine, it is just right to be topped up should I become thirsty or if someone offers to buy me another drink, or quickly emptied should some free champagne suddenly appear.'

Nigel prepares himself for opportunity to come knocking

Feeling good after getting to grips with his major issue and the successful deployment of the cunning plan, Nigel went back to his copy of the book that had inspired that very plan of such extreme cunningness and urged him to confront his challenges. He completed the versatility exercise and realised that his

---

2. Apologies to all management consultants – I was one once as well (but I'm OK now). There are some more definitions in the appendices that insult other professions as well – I like to offer a balance.

flexibility was closer to rigor mortis than anything else. Changes were indeed needed.

Nigel understood that he needed to be efficient in the way he worked and, as ever with Nigel, there was a joke about efficiency savings in the back of his mind.

An efficiency expert concluded his lecture with a note of caution. 'Don't try these techniques at home.'

'Why not?' asked somebody from the audience.

'I watched my wife's routine at breakfast for years,' the expert explained. 'She made lots of trips between the fridge, stove, table and cabinets, often carrying a single item at a time. One day I told her 'You're wasting too much time my dear. Why don't you try carrying several things at once?'

'Did it save time?' the guy in the audience asked.

'Actually, yes,' replied the expert. 'It used to take her twenty minutes to make breakfast. Now I do it in ten.'

Looking at his self-assessment his eye was immediately drawn to the number of hours that he spent on emails each day. He remembered being on a course sometime in the past at which the trainer commented, 'If you have to scroll you have lost control.' In this case Nigel knew that he had far too many emails and as a result he was not in control, he was sure to miss some important things that were bound to come back to bite him at some future point.

Nigel made a decision. First thing tomorrow he would focus on getting his inbox down in size and to question each email he received that day to see if he really needed to get involved in the chain or not.

He thought 'If you have to scroll you have lost control', would make an interesting sign for his desk.

'Stay committed to your decisions, but stay flexible in your approach.'

Tom Robbins

Are we there yet?

In which, having made the commitment to yes, we learn to consider the most appropriate path forward in order to deliver the sweet spot of effort – that point where the maximum value has been delivered for the optimum effort.

As a small child, I could never understand why we seemed to drive for so long in the family car to get somewhere special for a day out. As the minutes and sometimes hours were consumed in travel I would look out of my window and see interesting place after interesting place go by. What was wrong with stopping at that park? That wood? That river? Why did we have to keep going to the specific destination of parental choice?

In the end we always arrived somewhere good and had a great day out but I would have been just as happy (or so I thought) stopping earlier and enduring less 'car time'.

My perceived 'point of success' as far as a day out was concerned was a whole lot earlier than my parents.[1] Who knows, maybe I've always been lazy (in a good way of course).

But we have now reached the last two of the five key questions[2] set at the beginning of this book:

---

1. As the dedication at the start of this book reveals, my parents have now abandoned the car in favour of the aeroplane – the trips out continue but to further reaches these days (and I am no longer invited).
2. Remember earlier on in the book (Decision time) you needed to answer all of my questions? I knew that you were thinking, 'Did he ask six questions or only five?' Well what do you think now?

- If you have to do it then what is the shortest path to the point of success?
- What exactly is that point of success and at what stage will you just be wasting your time?

If you have to do it and you want to do it then what is it that you actually have to do? What is the shortest path to the point of success? We are all driven by the desire to do a great job if at all possible but there is a difference between delivering to the task and delivering beyond the task. Performance over and beyond the call of duty can be appropriate in some cases, particularly if you are dealing with someone for the first time perhaps and trying to win them over in some way, but in most cases it isn't appropriate or beneficial to anyone.

What is the shortest acceptable path?

What is the earliest point of success?

How do you go about identifying exactly that point of success beyond which you will just be wasting your time?

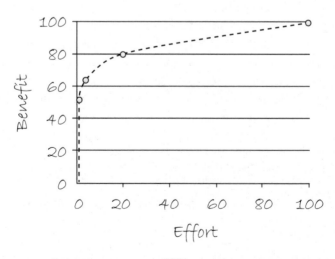

What you need to do is identify the 'sweet spot' which can be defined as the point where the cumulative return of your personal effort outweighs the benefit of the enhanced deliverable. There is an average guide to aid you here – the good old 80/20 rule is back in action and showing the way.

Yes, 20% of the effort delivers 80% of the benefit.

Easy! Well maybe so, but do your homework here and make sure that in each situation or case the 80% benefit is safe and suitable.

All you have to do is decide if that 80% benefit is enough for the purposes of this specific task or not, and if not, what percentage will be. What will drive this decision will include:

- Quality standards, safety standards, legal requirements or other rigid governance protocols.

Assuming that we are not talking about such matters this decision will be driven by:

Personal satisfaction. What level will you put on the satisfaction limit – the danger here is to over-deliver just because you enjoy doing the activity, which is all well and good if you have the time available but not productive if you don't.

Desire to please. How much are you trying to satisfy others? This may be a regular job that can be done to an acceptable level and people will be happy or this may be a situation when you really want to impress.

Try to find the 'sweet spot' every time you engage in an activity; it should be part of the planning stage of everything you do.

Don't over-engineer it – don't over-resource it – don't over-complicate it – and don't overdo what only needs to be done to the level of 'just enough'.

But don't cut corners either.

Don't waste your valuable time in correcting mistakes – avoid the mistakes in the first place.

Repetition of tasks, completing recovery work, duplication of effort – all waste time and are counterproductive – so why take that path when you are striving to be efficient in everything else you do? There is little value in working towards a focused and simple 'to do' list only to increase the required effort of each task through sloppy low quality work which will push you back up to your maximum capacity once again. Pointless!

Nigel understands the sweet spot

Over a coffee, he was not sure which number this was in the day but it wasn't the first, or the second, or the third or fourth that was for sure, Nigel had a moment of inspiration.

He decided there and then to put together a proposal to his boss about his great idea. He was particularly excited about this as not only was the idea a good one but he never normally had time for ideas as such. Something must be working.

Talking to a colleague who Nigel had decided to trust with his big idea, the conversation turned to how much detail Nigel should put in the proposal and when to talk to his boss about it. Nigel was immediately thinking he needed to put a whole lot of his newly acquired spare time into this and do some solid research before setting up the meeting. His colleague suggested that this was not the best way.

'Just spend some time thinking this one through and try to deal with all of the angles and make sure you have the basic answers ready if you are challenged,' was the advice. 'Then, assuming the idea is greeted positively, you can agree with the boss to allocate some of your work time to taking this to the next stage.'

This made sense to Nigel. Not only could he set up the meeting that much quicker but he could, if all went well, avoid having to do a lot of the work in his own time. A real win-win when he thought about it.

Nigel thanked his coach and got to it. He might actually have some time this weekend to finally dig out his golf clubs from the garage.

Nigel does play golf … rarely. He never seemed to have the time in the past, but he understands the concept of the sweet spot when it comes to making contact between the golf club and the ball.

Nigel had many, many golfing jokes but they were all so terrible that he really didn't want to share them with anyone.

Change

'If you think you can
or you think you can't,
either way you are right.'

Henry Ford

Escaping the comfort zone

In which the desire for change is compared to the resistance to change, that which holds us back from making any significant adjustments to the way we are and the way we work, in order to find the right combination to achieve escape velocity.

It is important to understand the balance of change if you indeed want to change your ways to those of a lazy winner.

Without reaching some sort of 'escape velocity' (as in space flight[1]) you will never do anything different. Deciding to be different or to bring about some form of change is most often easiest done when you have no choice in the matter, when outside forces[2] give you no option other than to change. But we are talking here about reaching the point of conscious decision to make a personal change.

Look at it this way.

---

1. In physics, escape velocity is the speed at which the kinetic energy plus the gravitational potential energy of an object is zero. It is the speed needed to 'break free' from a gravitational field without further propulsion. The term 'escape velocity' is actually a misnomer, as the concept refers to a scalar speed which is independent of direction whereas velocity is the measurement of the rate and direction of change in position of an object.
2. Part of the reason that I finally became an author came as a result of life circumstances forcing me to review how I was working. That and some advice from an external influencer that I should think about having more than one 'string to my bow' in the future. (A person who has more than one string to their bow has different talents or skills to fall back on.)

Change can be described as C(urrent), that is where you are now, and D(esire), where you want to be and B(enefit), which is the resultant reward for whatever change is undertaken.

For example...

Effect: My house feels crowded and noisy, and on top of that I have nowhere to put things... And this is making life less pleasant!

This can be described as: My current house is too small (C), I would like a bigger house (D), the benefit of having a bigger house would be more room for me and my family (B).

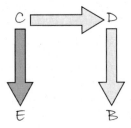

E (ffects) are also important because they will force a change

Now you may be in a number of states as far as change is concerned:

- You may lack any insight to your problems or need to change (unlikely that – you are here because you have invested in a book to help you bring about some form of life change. Or perhaps someone bought this book for you, in which case maybe they have some insight into your needs).
- You may have insight but need a solution or plan (well hopefully this is the book to help you out).
- You may have a plan but need some assistance in making it happen.

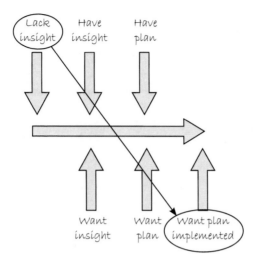

For example…

- Lack of insight – Why does my house seem so crowded and noisy, with nowhere to put things?
- Insight but no plan – My house is too small what shall I do?
- Insight and plan – My house is too small, I need to move, how will I do this?

Warning: we are about to head off into science again.

For change	Against change
Needs	Cost
Problems	Risk
Benefits	Pain
Implications	Hidden

Against change

To move anyone towards change there is a balancing act that needs to be performed. There are a number of resistances that stop change taking place, or at least allow you to put up personal arguments against changing (these might be those small voices in your head that you hear from time to time):

Cost. Everything has a perceived cost whether this is actual money that would need to be invested or just your time and effort (and distraction from other matters).

Risk. A concern over what such change would bring about should it in some way fail and require recovery, the work to be redone or loss of face. Concern about the risk of failure and what that would mean to you and others.

Pain. Recognition that change usually means some form of pain that needs to be endured, the negative aspects of the process of change itself.

Hidden. It is often possible to uncover the first three points but there will often remain 'hidden' reasons that someone is resistant to such change. If this is yourself then it is a matter of being honest with yourself, if this is you looking to assess the desire for change in others then this is harder to understand.

This makes it hard to assess the 'balance' of resistance since while it may be possible to quantify and address the 'cost', 'risk' and 'pain' elements the 'hidden' ones remain hidden and therefore un-quantifiable.

For change

On the other side of the balancing scales are the reasons for change:

Needs. The definable drivers for adopting a process of change, the need of the person to make a change.

Problems. What is it that is causing some issue or concern in the status quo that offers the desire to make some form of change?

Benefits. What are the desirable benefits of such change, the expected beneficial outcomes of adopting something new?

Implications. If no change is initiated then what will the impact be, what will the consequences be? The implication being that something must be encouraging the need for change in the first place.

Therefore, you need to make sure that the scales fall more heavily on the side of 'for change' in order to stand a chance of making such change a reality.

Formula for change

There is another formula that applies here as well. The Formula for Change was created by Richard Beckhard and David Gleicher, refined by Kathie Dannemiller and is sometimes called Gleicher's Formula.[3] This formula (D x V x F x CL > R) provides a model for assessing the relative strengths affecting the likely success or otherwise of organisational change programmes.

---

3. The original formula, as created by Gleicher and authored by Beckhard and Harris, is: C = (ABD) > X where C is change, A is the status quo dissatisfaction, B is a desired clear state, D is practical steps to the desired state, and X is the cost of the change. It was Kathleen Dannemiller who dusted off the formula and simplified it, making it more accessible for consultants and managers.

Three factors must be present for meaningful organisational change to take place. These factors are:

D = Dissatisfaction with how things are now
V = Vision of what is possible
F = First, concrete steps that can be taken towards the vision
CL = Creative Leadership to navigate towards the vision

If the product of these four factors is greater than

R = Resistance

then change is possible. Because D, V, and F are multiplied, if any one of them is absent or low, then the product will be low and therefore not capable of overcoming the resistance.

To ensure a successful change it is necessary to use influence and strategic thinking in order to create vision and identify those crucial, early steps towards it. In addition, the organisation must recognise and accept the dissatisfaction that exists by communicating industry trends, leadership ideas, best practice and competitive analysis to identify the necessity for change.

'Change is inevitable – except from a vending machine.'

Robert C. Gallagher

Dealing with change

This is a book about change but it is not actually a book teaching personal change theory. That said, as an overview or high level appreciation of what we as individuals typically experience when faced with change, John Fisher's[4] model of personal change is a good one. He suggests that we may experience different emotions at different stages of the change process, including:

- Anxiety – The awareness that events lie outside our range of understanding or control.
- Happiness – The awareness that our viewpoint is recognised and shared by others.
- Fear – The awareness of an imminent incidental change in our core behavioural system.
- Threat – The awareness of an imminent comprehensive change in our core behavioural structure.
- Guilt – Awareness of dislodgement of self from our core self-perception.
- Depression – This phase is characterised by a general lack of motivation and confusion.
- Disillusionment – The awareness that our values, beliefs and goals are incompatible with those around us.
- Hostility – Continued effort to validate social predictions that have already proved to be a failure.

---

4. Originally presented at the Tenth International Personal Construct Congress, Berlin, 1999, and subsequently developed in his work on constructivist theory in relation to service provision organisations at Leicester University, England, John Fisher's model of personal change – *The Transition Curve* – is an excellent analysis of how individuals deal with personal change. This model is an extremely useful reference for individuals dealing with personal change and for managers and organisations helping staff to deal with personal change.

- Denial – Lack of acceptance of any change and denial that there will be any impact on us an individual.

OK, science bit over – you can relax again.

All in all it is quite a lot to take in, I know, but just focus on this: small incremental changes work best (with some sort of vision of where you want to go) and tend to hurt less, worry you less, and cost you less. Typically they do not put too much 'weight' on the 'against change' side of the scales.

Make the change through small incremental steps

Nigel makes a momentous decision

Pleased as he was with his recent 'successes' Nigel was still working long hours and spending insufficient time at home with his family and relaxing.

He did now have a vision of where he wanted to be in a few weeks, a few months and within a year, and he had already experienced the benefit of asking for help along the way from colleagues. His challenge was a classic one, the 'what comes first' challenge – how can you really apply changes when you are already busy? And how can you stop being busy in order to apply changes?

Nigel knows a joke about solving the problem of priorities.

Question: Which came first, the chicken or the egg?

Answer: A hen is only an egg's way of making another egg.

This is one of Nigel's more subtle jokes.

Nigel knows another joke about which came first, the chicken or the egg,[5] but he is not allowed to tell this one in polite company and it is not one of Nigel's more subtle jokes.

After thinking all this through for a while Nigel came to the conclusion that what he was experiencing was a degree of resistance to change. He looked at the cost – risk – pain – hidden 'against change' section in the book once more.

His mind focused on the 'risk' element, 'the recognition that change usually means some form of pain that needs to be endured, the negative aspects of the process of change itself'.

Nigel came to the conclusion that he needed to deal with his backlog of work. He was being careful about saying 'yes' these days and he was frugal in the efforts he was putting into the work that he was undertaking, without compromising the needed quality of course. So he would address his challenge in two ways. He declared to his family that for the next two weeks he would, as a one-off exercise, work even harder – he explained what he was trying to achieve and asked for their help and understanding. Secondly, he would look at each and every task and, with tough honesty, cut tasks down in size and scale and stop working on the ones which he could realistically leave unfinished or incomplete. In these cases he would explain to each affected person what he was doing and, again, ask for their help and understanding.

In summary he would 'take some pain to make some gain' but only for a short, fixed period of time.

---

5. The real answer to this age-old conundrum can be found in the appendices. If you want to hear the other joke that Nigel knows you will just have to buy him a beer when he is not in polite company.

The influence of five and the relationship of six

In which we look at the ways that you can be influenced and how to gain the most advantage from those both close to you and also slightly further away in your network of opportunity. Surprisingly perhaps, that network is a lot bigger and nearer than you may think.

In order to be different in some way and change from what you are, or were if you have started already, then you will definitely need some help (beyond a good book and guide like *The lazy winner*) along the way.

Here are two ways to understand what and who around you offers influence, good or not so good, and how to adjust your current network of influence to help you achieve what you wish to achieve.

When I reflect back I can see that many people have influenced me over the years but mostly I didn't realise it at the time.

'You don't have to be a "person of influence" to be influential. In fact, the most influential people in my life are probably not even aware of the things they've taught me.'

Scott Adams

The influence of five

It is said that we are the average of the five people we most closely associate with.[1] So, if you are one of those five people closest to others then you have a great opportunity to promote yourself, your personal desires, and your work. If you present enthusiasm at all (reasonable) times then you really can influence others around you. It is also said that enthusiasm is contagious (but so is the lack of it) so be careful and be positive. At all times, even the difficult times, present what you are trying to achieve in a way that is:

- **Positive** – as we have seen your enthusiasm can be infectious and engaging with people about the positive aspects of what you, and they, are doing can only be a good thing.
- **Good for everyone involved** – listen to people's views and try to identify the challenges that others face that you may be able to address or help with.
- **The right thing to do** – talk about the 'greater good' for everyone involved or associated with the change.

Of course you need to keep an open mind and be seen as someone who does consider the views of others.

Consider yourself as the extra one to the five as well. By that I mean it is not just a matter of you being freely influenced by others around you, there is a strong connection to your spirit, personality and strength of character as to how much you are influenced, and indeed how much you influence others.

Now you might consider, as you want to change in some positive way, assessing your own 'relationship of five'. Who are they? Are

---

1. 'You are the average of the five people you spend the most time with,' suggested Jim Rohn, motivational speaker and self-help guru. Jim Rohn (1930–2009) was an American entrepreneur, author and motivational speaker. His rags to riches story played a large part in his work, which influenced others in the personal development industry.

these the best influencers to aid your journey? Who could you connect with in order to help you further?

Try this assessment right now:

Question: Who are the five people you spend the most time with in your life[2] right now?

- What are they like?
- What are their top three qualities?
- What proportion of your time do you spend with them?

OK good, now try this:

Question: What is it that you would like to change?

- What is the ideal that you wish to become?
- What are the qualities you want to possess?
- Where will your journey take you?

And finally:

- Do the five people you are now connected to most closely match who you want to become in the future?

To be clear, I am not suggesting dumping those around you and going cold-heartedly out to find five new (better) relationships – absolutely not. I am just suggesting that change is easier when you are well supported in this process. If you are constantly surrounded by negative, fear-based people in your life, it will have an impact on who you eventually become and your progression in life.

Here's another question, well a question in two parts actually.

---

2. I would focus on adults here although it is surprising how influential your children can be.

Question: Among those people that you know, who is the number one person you would aspire to be like, who embodies what it is that you would like to change?

Question: Among those people that you know of who is the number one person you would aspire to be like, who embodies what it is that you would like to change? The difference with this question is that you can pick anybody at all – even though you might not know them. They may or may not be famous. They may or may not be alive. They may be anyone, anywhere.

Now for the first person consider how you would get closer to them, to be influenced more by them, make them become one of your five influencers.

And for the person that you only know of, but do not have contact with, how can you get closer to them in some way?

Well you could try contacting them; you never know what might happen. Most people now have in place some means of communicating with them (or their representatives) through email, social networks, websites, letters, phone calls and so on.

If direct contact doesn't work out for you then you can always effectively engage with the essence of that person in the form of their works: books, blogs, articles, webcasts, training courses or materials, presentations that you could attend or listen to recordings of, television shows or radio shows, or any other way that you can make an indirect connection.

The relationship of six

A 'degree of separation' is a measure of social distance between people. You are one degree away from everyone you know, two degrees away from everyone they know, and so on.[3] Think of it as a vast spider web connecting you in some way to everyone else.

A personal network then is a set of human contacts known to an individual, with whom that individual would expect to interact at intervals to support a given set of activities. That status of 'knowing' does not necessarily mean that there is deep knowledge or understanding between the parties involved, rather that they are connected in some way and have some form of mutual interest or background.

Personal networks are intended to be mutually beneficial – extending the concept of teamwork beyond the immediate peer group. The term is often encountered in the workplace, though these days it could apply equally to other pursuits outside work. Such networking is usually undertaken over an extended period and, these days, there are many technology based means to aid such networking – connecting, tracking, updating, sharing and communicating – and to scale networks in a global fashion.[4]

It could be through such a network that you could in fact reach out and connect to that person that you would like to have as one of your influencers but that you only know of.

One of the great lessons I have learned as I have personally explored building my networks is that, for the greater part, people

---

3. Six degrees of separation (also referred to as the 'human spider web') refers to the idea that everyone is, on average, approximately six steps away from any other person on Earth, so that a chain of, 'a friend of a friend' statements can be made, on average, to connect any two people in six steps or fewer. It was originally set out by Frigyes Karinthy and popularised in a play written by John Guare.

4. I am not going to list them here, you all know what they are, but I am on most of them so feel free to connect. I am not promising to be a good influencer for you but I am happy to share my network to our mutual advantage if possible.

are happy and willing to help out. Of course you have to be ready to reciprocate, that is how it all works. I have been surprised many times over at how quickly I can contact someone I wanted to reach – other authors and speakers, many of whom I had been fans of for some time – and at how willing they all were to communicate with me and aid me.

Start thinking about who you would like to connect with, why this is so, and how they might help you (and be ready to offer your help in return). Who do you now know who might start you on the path to connection with your end target?

Influencers

By considering who is now influencing you and who would better influence you, you can, in some way, bring about a change through other people.

Who are your influencers and how can you gather more influencers to help you out?

The journey is always easier with others by your side and ready to give you a positive comment or a guiding suggestion.

Nigel makes some new friends

Nigel is enjoying a cappuccino in his local coffee shop. It had been a tough two long weeks, in fact just over two weeks in the end, but he felt he had achieved something very positive.

Tonight, as a thank you to his family for their support and encouragement, he is taking them all out for a steak meal and no doubt a glass or two of wine. And now, as a reward for himself, he is taking some time out to read the book once again. The section on influence was very interesting and Nigel reflected back on the guidance he had gained on the big idea at work from an influential colleague. That was a good influence and had paid off dividends.

A smile came to his lips as Nigel remembered a joke about the expected benefits of influence and the potential downside when it doesn't go as expected.

A lady approaches the priest in her parish and tells him about a problem that she has.

'Father, I have a problem. I have been given these two wonderful talking female parrots but they only know how to say one thing.'

'What is it that they say then?' enquired the priest.

'They only know how to say, "Hi, we're prostitutes. Do you want to have some fun?"'

'That is terrible!' the priest exclaimed. 'But I have a solution to your problem. Bring your two talking female parrots over to my house and I will put them with my two male talking parrots. I have taught them to pray and read the Bible. My parrots will teach your parrots to stop saying that terrible phrase and your female parrots will learn to praise and worship the Lord.'

'Oh thank you!' responded the woman.

So the next day, the lady brings her female parrots to the priest's house. The priest's two male parrots are holding rosary beads and praying in their cage. The lady puts her female parrots in with the male parrots and she and the priest leave them alone.

An hour later, after a cup of tea, the two return to the room only to hear the female parrots say.

'Hi, we're prostitutes. Do you want to have some fun?'

One male parrot looks over at the other male parrot and exclaims: 'Put the Bibles away. Our prayers have been answered!'

Nigel almost laughed out loud when he recalled this joke but stifled it instead and took another sip of his coffee.

Tonight, he thought, he would consider the influencers in his life and make some more plans. No, correction – tomorrow he would do that, tonight was family time.

Momentum

'It's not that I'm so smart, it's just that I stay with problems longer.'

Albert Einstein

When the going gets tough

In which the reality of hitting the occasional brick wall and losing the way is openly acknowledged, and some ideas on how to get past the moment when things get a little tough[1] are shared.

The path to productive laziness will not necessarily be a smooth one.

When you hit the wall

It is possible that despite all of this thinking and planning and focusing, the clear plan of action, the short and pertinent 'to do' list you might hit the wall of inaction, the quicksand of apathy, the jungle of procrastination. And you stop.

If this happens here are two tips that may get you moving:

1. Read *Eat that Frog!* by Brian Tracy (easy, insightful and useful).[2]
   The key to reaching high levels of performance and productivity

---

1. 'When the going gets tough, the tough get going' is a popular saying. The phrase has been attributed both to Joseph P. Kennedy, father of the US President John F. Kennedy, and to Norwegian-born American football player and coach, Knute Rockne. A song of the same name was recorded by Billy Ocean in 1985.
2. In his book *Eat That Frog!* author Brian Tracy helps you to stop procrastinating and be more effective in managing your time. The key to reaching high levels of performance and productivity is to develop the lifelong habit of tackling your major task first thing each morning. There's an old saying that if you eat a live frog in the morning, nothing worse can happen for the rest of the day. Your 'frog' should be the most difficult item on your to-do list.

is to develop the lifelong habit of tackling your major task first thing each morning.

2. Go and do something completely different. Go with what really gets you going, what truly excites you. If you are uninspired to do something then it is probably because that something seems very boring to you. If so, move on to something that doesn't seem so boring, something far more exciting. Come up with a list of things you could do that are important and productive and still exciting and go with those tasks. You will be avoiding something boring for sure, but you will be motivated to do the other, more exciting stuff. And when you have regained your energy and enthusiasm you will often find that you tackle the boring stuff with enthusiasm and success – you just needed to get motivated.

Interestingly I have found, many times over, that even when you hit that 'wall' and go off and do something more exciting, the something else that you have done turns out to be useful pretty soon afterwards. I am not sure if this is because you tend to do things that you know in the back of your mind might be useful or relevant, or you think in terms of 'how can I reuse that great stuff I put together a while ago' when problem solving, or maybe a combination of both.

Either way it does seem that very little of what I do, even in these moments of re-motivation, ends up being wasted.

Go with the pulse

The question of single or multi-tasking might also arise. In reality we can't survive without multi-tasking (even the men). I mean, if all we could cope with was 'breathe in, breathe out' then that would pretty much wipe out the whole self-help book genre, among a lot of other things.

But which approach delivers the best progress?

We spoke earlier about the whole 'more haste, less speed' principle that makes us, when we are in a hurry, more often end up completing the task in a slower time, due to making mistakes on the way and having to rework stuff or put in recovery effort.

We also covered the fact that, typically, only 20% of what you do really matters because it is that effort that delivers 80% of the results required. Linked to that you should therefore allow yourself to concentrate and focus on the really important stuff at times. So I would suggest that it is perfectly acceptable in these situations to single task; not all of the time obviously, but when something is that important then you don't want any distractions.

The rest of the time it is definitely multi-tasking all the way. But consider this: although multi-tasking does have its benefits, there are times when it can get a bit overwhelming. Taking on a lot of work you tend to spread yourself too thinly and the law of diminishing returns begins to take effect.

I find that my efficiency rises with the more work I do, within reason, and drops as tasks get longer and more detailed. Therefore I approach work in a series of 'pulses' doing a little here and a little there that all add up to a final result or delivery. Taking this approach keeps me fresh and alert, interested and focused, and allows me to effectively 'prototype' small packets of effort to identify the best outcome or solution. When something doesn't work then I haven't wasted whole heaps of time and I can easily redirect my efforts and stay positive.

'Every day may not be good, but there's something good in every day.'

Unknown

Nigel just does it

It has all been going so well for Nigel recently. Progress was being made in both reducing the workload he took on board and in the delivery of the work that he had committed to. He had looked carefully at all of his influencers and he was working on maximising the impact of both those close to hand and at a further distance.

And then he hit the wall. Now he was used to this feeling from many experiences of 'wall hitting' in the past but for some reason, maybe because he was feeling more in control these days, this one hurt a lot more!

Time to reach for the book again and sure enough this had been covered in *The lazy winner* in the section on 'Momentum'. Here Nigel found guidance on the subject of eating frogs, and he also found a lot more advice that was equally encouraging in his current predicament.

Nigel finished reading and with a smile on his face stood up and went outside.

Thirty minutes later he returned, still with a big smile on his face. Looking out of his window he could see his car shining in the sun, clean and bright, with a pool of drying water on the ground. Refreshed from some air and a sense of a job well done for 'me, me, me', Nigel put the kettle on and thought about his difficult task again. He had been so lost in the act of cleaning his car, with the music playing loudly, that he had not thought about the problem for most of the time he had been outside.

A joke had been on his mind though.

An elderly lady had stopped to drive her car into a parking space when a young man in his brand new red sports car drove around her and parked in the space that she had been waiting for. She was so angered that she approached the young fellow and said, through gritted teeth, 'I was about to park there! Why did you do that?'

The man looked at her with disdain and replied, 'That's what you can do when you're young and bright.'

This annoyed the elderly lady even more and so she got back in her car, backed it up, and then stamped on the accelerator and rammed straight into his car.

The young man ran back to his car and shouted in a stunned voice, 'What did you do that for?'

She smiled at him and said 'That's what you can do when you're old and rich.'

Nigel smiled again, always good to know your strengths and weaknesses in any situation.

Now, as the kettle boiled a thought suddenly struck him that might just get him started again on that tricky problem.

Destination

You have reached your destination

Only you will know what your destination is, based on the work that you did at the start of the book.

Have you reached it?

Have you at least started out on the journey?

You are here

I joked that you could think of this book as the 'sat nav' for your journey for change.

Well these days I use a satellite navigation system in my own car. Not all of the time though since it is not built into the old Saab that I drive but has to be stuck on the windscreen and connected to the power from the lighter socket. So '2006' I know, but that's just the way it is.

But it is a comfort and I do enjoy the calm, unruffled and dispassionate advice that she hands out to me by voice and by graphical display.

I say 'she' of course since I have selected the voice of 'Carol'. My wife on the other hand has selected 'Ken' the Australian for some bizarre reason. Each to their own is all I can say.

The old days of map reading and general direction guidance was an instant recipe for marital strife since neither the driver nor the guide could ever agree on the need for information, the speed of supply of this information, the accuracy of the information, or anything really. A simple trip to a new location for a convivial lunch with relatives or the delivery of a small child to the house of a new friend could escalate the likelihood of divorce proceedings being initiated as easily as match ignites dynamite.

These days it is so much better. 'Carol' (let's assume that I am driving) asks me where I want to go, and when, and then breaks the route down into small steps or stages and off we go. The great thing is that when 'Carol' is wrong (I do occasionally obviously know better that her and her satellite friend) and I drive past the turning she politely asked me to take she quietly acknowledges my superior intelligence with the phrase 'recalculating' and then gives me the right directions. She can be wrong, but just appreciates the lessons learned and recalculates. I am told that 'Ken' does this as well.

Conversely the mere hint that I might not manage to take that sharp left that was announced to me a massive twenty-five metres before the actual turning by my human navigator can result in three weeks of subsequent marital silence.

So it is clear to me that it is the calm and assured leader who gets you from 'A' to 'B' in the most effective way.

Following instructions blindly teaches you nothing.

Now, great as my 'sat nav' can be it has one huge drawback. If I follow the instructions once to find my 'B' then I will most likely not be able to find it a second time through my own devices. I will need 'Carol' the second time as well, and the third.

I will need a guide each and every time unless I look up and do it myself at some point.

The real art here is to learn what you need to learn and then make it your own. It is your 'change', your 'journey', your 'life', so take what you need from this book and adapt it all to turn yourself into the 'winner' that you want to be, the lazy winner hopefully.

A lazy, lazy winner

In which the author tries to make this as easy as possible in order to satisfy his own desire to be productively lazy in everything he does, as well as helping others to be the same.

I always try and make things as simple as possible, hopefully I have succeeded so far, but here (as ever to aid you on your journey to productive laziness) is a shortened list of what I have talked about in this book, a real lazy 'lazy' guide.

Use this once you have defined your own 'winning' goals and plotted your journey of change of course.

It is always good to have a quick reference.[1]

Ask yourself some fundamental questions

Do I want to do this piece of work, job or task? Even if I do want to do it, do I need to do it?

- Don't do something just because everyone else does it or because it is the 'usual thing to do'.
- Ask: 'Is this really necessary?' and 'Is this really worth doing?'
- If the answer is 'no' then don't do it.

---

1. If anyone asks you later on, this chapter is available on its own (but it is the same price as the book!).

Is the result or outcome worth my effort?
- Only do the things with the most impact.
- Your time is limited so invest it only in things that give you the most return on your personal investment.

Do I have to do this myself?
- Ask yourself if you really are the best possible person to do whatever it is that needs to be done.
- Is there someone else in your network who is better qualified than you to do this thing?
- If there is then be generous and let them help you out.

If you have to do it, then what is the shortest path to the point of success?
- Don't waste your time on the unnecessary. If it works in black and white don't waste effort in creating a Technicolor dream version of the same thing.
- Do only the things that are necessary to get the job done.
- Cut everything else out!

What exactly is that point of success and at what stage will you just be wasting your time?
- Can this be reused again and again?
- Can it have more value than just a 'one-off' piece of work?
- If it can then scale it for better return on investment.

Think – Plan – Prioritise – Focus

And if you do decide that you need and want to do something:
- Can you automate it? Can you scale it? Can you make it reusable in a wider context?
- Can you simplify it? Can you shorten it?

- Can it wait? Is it really needed when it is supposed to be needed? Will it impact on others if it waits?

Getting 'yes' and 'no' in balance

Say 'no' when that is the right answer.
- It is all about balance and priority. Overall you want to deal with the important stuff plus a reasonable amount of other stuff.
- If you keep saying 'yes' then your backlog will never go down and you will spend far too much time working on the unimportant.

And say 'yes' when that is the right answer.
- Only 20% of what you do really matters – so focus on that!
- Available to Promise – a qualified 'yes'.
- Can you do even more if you wait a little while longer?

Plan to your own capacity

100% is not a good thing.

If you don't keep 20% of your available time free you won't:
- Be able to deal with sudden issues.
- Be able to take advantage of new opportunities.

Test your own capacity now – and test it again in a few weeks' time to track your progress.

Finding the best path

If you have to do something then what is the shortest path to the point of success?

What exactly is that point of success and at what stage will you just be wasting your time?

Find your 'sweet spot' – every time. Don't over-engineer, don't over-resource, don't over-do what only needs to be done 'just enough'.

Do it right first time

But don't cut corners.

Repetition of tasks, completing recovery work, duplication of effort – all waste time and are counterproductive – so why take that path?

Be effective and be efficient.

Influencers

Give yourself the very best chance of success by surrounding yourself with good influencers.
- Look at the five closest to you – and influence your own influencers.
- Look beyond your close circle and build your network.
- Be generous to your own network – give in order to receive.[2]

2. Copies of *The lazy winner* would be a great start to the whole giving thing.

Don't panic

If you hit the 'wall' don't worry.

- Go off and do other things, come back to the task when your mind is refreshed.
- Pulse work – short, sharp inputs of effort to keep your mind active.

Whatever you work on at any time will have some value in the future – nothing is wasted.

Whatever happened to Nigel?

Nigel really felt that he had come a long way in a short time.

Just by having matters laid out for him, literally in black and white, he could see how he himself could take some degree of control and improve things. None of the steps were too challenging and he could see small successes each step of the way as he progressed from chapter to chapter.

Just so that he didn't regress from his personal journey he had copied out the lazy, lazy winner tips and had them on his office wall. In fact this initiated more than one conversation on the topic of productive laziness with visitors to his office, conversations that he enjoyed a lot now that he felt he was a real lazy winner.

And yes we shouldn't at all be surprised that Nigel does have a joke ready.

A young man was keen to find out how he could become successful as quickly as possible and so he found an older man who had become a success in his work and life.

'Sir, what is the secret of your success?' he asked.

'Two words,' came the response.

'And, Sir, what are they?' asked the young man excitedly.

'Right decisions.'

The young man wrote this down with enthusiasm.

'And how do you make right decisions?'

'One word,' responded the older man.

'And, Sir, what is that?' asked the young man.

'Experience.'

The young man noted this as well and asked his next question.

'And how do you get experience?'

'Two words,' smiled the older man.

'And, Sir, what are they?' questioned the young man.

'Wrong decisions.'

Nigel couldn't understand why some people didn't get his sense of humour. Maybe there was another self-help book out there that could help him?[3] Or better still a self-help book he could suggest to others.

But one thing was clear in Nigel's mind: this was all working because he was clear about what he wanted to change in his life and why he wanted to change it. Change without purpose and clarity is a wasted effort. He believed in the productive lazy approach and had proved that it worked for him and that he could work with it, through small simple steps.

Thinking about why he had set out on this journey in the first place he remembered another story about a simple fisherman who was offered opportunity through change.

---

3. Perhaps *How to get paid more, laid more, live a longer, happier life and develop a respectable sense of humour* is a step too far for any self-help book?

A man was on vacation and was standing at the pier of a small island village when a small boat with just one fisherman docked.

Inside the small boat were several large grouper. The man complimented the islander on the quality of his fish and asked how long it took to catch them.

The islander replied: 'Only a little while.'

The man considered for a while and then asked the fisherman why didn't he stay out longer and catch more fish?

The islander said he had enough to support his family's immediate needs.

The man then thought some more before he asked 'But what do you do with the rest of your time?'

The fisherman said 'I sleep late, fish a little, play with my children, take a late afternoon nap with my wife, stroll into the village each evening where I sip rum and play guitar with my friends, I have a full and busy life.'

The man scoffed at this answer and said 'I am a professional man with an MBA and many years of experience and I could help you.'

The fisherman looked puzzled and asked the man how he could help.

'You should spend more time fishing and, with the proceeds, buy a bigger boat. Then with the proceeds from the bigger boat you could buy several boats. Eventually you would have a fleet of fishing boats. Instead of selling your catch to a middleman you would sell directly to the processor, eventually opening your own cannery. You would control the product, processing and distribution. You would, of course, need to leave this small fishing village and move to the city to run your expanding enterprise,' declared the man with authority.

The fisherman asked 'But, how long will this all take?'

To which the man replied 'About fifteen to twenty years should do it I think.'

'But what then?' asked the fisherman.

The man laughed and said that this was the best part. 'When the time is right you would sell your company stock to the public and become very rich, you would make millions.'

'Millions, really? Then what?' questioned the villager.

The man thought for a short while and said, 'Then you would retire. Move to a small fishing village where you would sleep late, fish a little, play with your kids, take a late afternoon nap with your wife, stroll to the village in the evenings. Here you could sip rum and play your guitar with your friends.'

The fisherman smiled at the man and took his catch home.

The man stood looking confused for a while before he walked away from the pier.

Nigel laughed, he liked that joke. He stood up, put the *The lazy winner* back in his desk drawer and headed out of his office towards home.

As he did so he looked back at the new sign on his desk that said 'Progress isn't made by early risers. It's made by lazy men trying to find easier ways to do something.'[4]

---

4. This is the phrase that really summed up the whole 'lazy' and 'productive' idea for me, I am glad Nigel now thinks (and acts) the same way.

'If you always do what you always did, you'll always get what you always got.'

Unknown

A final thought

There was once a little bird who, though a very nice little bird, was also a very, very lazy little bird.

Every day, when it was time to get up, the other birds had to shout at him again and again before he would finally struggle out of bed. And when there was some job he had to do, he would keep putting it off until there was hardly enough time left to do it. His family and friends kept saying 'What a lazy bird you are! You can't just keep leaving everything to the last minute.'

'Bah! There's really no problem,' answered the little bird. 'I just take a bit longer to get around to doing things, that's all.'

The birds spent all summer flying and playing, and when the autumn came and they started feeling the cold, they began to prepare for the long journey to a warmer land. But our little bird, lazy as ever, kept putting it off, feeling quite sure that there was plenty of time. Until one day when he woke up and all the other birds were gone.

Just like every other day, several of his friends had tried to wake him, but – half asleep – he told them he would get up later. He had gone back to sleep and only woken up again much later. That day was the day of the great journey. Everyone knew the rules: you had to be ready to leave. There were thousands of birds, and they weren't going to wait around for anyone. So the little bird, who didn't know how to make the journey alone, realised that, because of his laziness, he would have to spend the long cold winter all on his own.

At the beginning, he spent a lot of time crying, but he had to admit that it was his own fault. He knew he could do things well when he put his mind to it so, putting his laziness aside, he began to prepare for the winter. First, he spent days looking for the place that was best protected from the cold. He found a place between some rocks, and there he made a new nest, well built with branches, stones and leaves. Then, he worked tirelessly to fill the nest with fruits and berries, enough to last the whole winter. Finally, he dug a little pool in the cave, so he would have enough water. When he saw that his new home was perfectly prepared, he began to train himself on how to get by on very little food and water, so that he would be able to endure the worst snowstorms.

And, although many would not have believed it possible, all these preparations meant that the little bird did survive through the winter. Of course, he suffered greatly, and not a day of that winter went by without him regretting having been such a lazy little bird. When the spring finally arrived, and his old friends returned from their voyage, they were all filled with joy and surprise at seeing that the little bird was still alive. They could hardly believe that such a lazy bird had managed to build such a wonderful nest. And when they realised that not even a bit of laziness remained in his little body, and that he had turned into the most hard-working bird of the flock, everyone agreed that he should be put in charge of organising the great journey the following year.

When that time came, everything was done so well and was so well prepared that they even had time left to invent an early morning wake-up song, so that from that day on no little bird, however lazy, would have to spend the winter alone again.

The little bird had learned from a costly error that working in a productive way was a better path to being 'lazy' in the sense that being prepared, being organised, and being focused on what you do leads you to a world of 'productive laziness' and indeed a better life.

Do you have time in your life to stop and listen to the birds singing in the trees occasionally?

More

Appendices

In which all the material that didn't fit into the main part of the book is stuffed at the end in case anyone wants to read some more (but you don't have to).

Decision time (five questions or six?)

I thought that it might be good to clear up the whole Dirty Harry/Clint Eastwood thing now, in case you were wondering and in case you cared. I said: 'I know what you're thinking, "did he ask six questions or only five?"'

Well, to tell you the truth, in all the excitement I kind of lost track myself. But being as this is a book about productive laziness, the most powerful way of working in the world, and could blow your head clean off, you've got to ask yourself one question: Do I feel lucky? Well, do ya?

Go ahead reader, make my day... or to be more precise, go ahead and make your day by learning to work in a better way, the winning way of productive laziness.

The answer (my answer is) – six. I asked six questions.

I asked the five key questions:

- Do you want to read *The lazy winner* and do you need to read *The lazy winner*?
- Will the outcome of reading *The lazy winner* be worth the effort?

- Do you have to read *The lazy winner* yourself?
- If you have to read *The lazy winner* then what is the shortest path to the point of success?
- What exactly is that point of success and at what stage will you just be wasting your time?

But then I also asked:
- So what is it going to be?

So reader, you were perfectly safe. I was clean out of questions. You were lucky (punk).

Why all the footnotes?

I like a book to flow easily and I like it to be as simple as possible to learn what I am hoping to learn without the distraction of detail or minutiae.

On the other hand I am one of those people who likes to pin down where a quote, a song lyric or a name comes from and where I might have heard the reference before.

So, as a result, you have the footnotes. Easy to ignore in order to get on with the whole productive laziness approach and yet helpfully there if you do need to put your mind at rest about something that has been referenced.

Too lazy to fail

Time Enough for Love is a science fiction novel by Robert A. Heinlein, first published in 1973. The work was nominated for the Nebula Award for Best Novel in 1973 and both the Hugo and Locus Awards in 1974.

The book covers several periods of the life of Lazarus Long (birth name Woodrow Wilson Smith), the oldest living human and now more than two thousand years old.

The first half of the book takes the form of several novellas tied together by Lazarus's retrospective narrative. In the framing story, Lazarus has grown weary and decided that life is no longer worth living, but (in what is described as a reverse Arabian Nights scenario) he will consent not to end his life as long as his companions will listen to his stories.

One is the story of 'The Man Who Was Too Lazy to Fail'. The story is just an aside about a boy who would do anything to get away from his parents' farm. He joined the navy, went to officer training and worked pretty hard, to the point that he retired as an admiral – all to get away from looking at 'the south end of a mule'. He did everything right the first time (after all, it's more work to get things wrong and have to correct them again than getting it right the first time around). He looked for the most efficient way to do everything, from flying airplanes to getting girls. All in all the character aspires to act in a 'constructively lazy' way.

Maslow

Maslow's hierarchy of needs is often portrayed in the shape of a pyramid, with the largest and most fundamental levels of needs at the bottom, and the need for self-actualisation at the top.

The most fundamental and basic four layers of the pyramid contain what Maslow called 'deficiency needs' or 'd-needs': esteem, friendship and love, security, and physical needs. With the exception of the most fundamental (physiological) needs, if these 'deficiency needs' are not met, the body gives no physical indication but the individual feels anxious and tense. Maslow's theory suggests that the most basic level of needs must be met before the individual will strongly desire (or focus motivation upon) the secondary or higher level needs. Maslow also coined the term 'Metamotivation' to describe the motivation of people who go beyond the scope of the basic needs and strive for constant betterment. Metamotivated people are driven by b-needs (being needs), instead of deficiency needs (d-needs).

Physiological needs

For the most part, physiological needs are obvious – they are literally the requirements for human survival. If these requirements are not met, the human body simply cannot continue to function.

Air, water, and food are metabolic requirements for survival in all animals, including humans. Clothing and shelter provide necessary protection from the elements. The intensity of the human sexual instinct is shaped more by sexual competition than maintaining a birth rate adequate to survival of the species.

Safety needs

With their physical needs relatively satisfied, the individual's safety needs take precedence and dominate behaviour. These needs have to do with people's yearning for a predictable orderly world in which perceived unfairness and inconsistency are under control, the familiar frequent and the unfamiliar rare. In the world of work, these safety needs manifest themselves in such things as a preference for job security, grievance procedures for protecting the individual from unilateral authority, savings accounts, insurance policies, reasonable disability accommodations, and the like.

Safety and security needs include:

• Personal security;
• Financial security;

- Health and well-being;
- Safety net against accidents/illness and their adverse impacts.

Love and belonging

After physiological and safety needs are fulfilled, the third layer of human needs are social and involve feelings of belongingness. This aspect of Maslow's hierarchy involves emotionally based relationships in general, such as:

- Friendship;
- Intimacy;
- Family.

Humans need to feel a sense of belonging and acceptance, whether it comes from a large social group, such as clubs, office culture, religious groups, professional organisations, sports teams, gangs, or small social connections (family members, intimate partners, mentors, close colleagues, confidantes). They need to love and be loved (sexually and non-sexually) by others. In the absence of these elements, many people become susceptible to loneliness, social anxiety, and clinical depression. This need for belonging can often overcome the physiological and security needs, depending on the strength of the peer pressure.

Esteem

All humans have a need to be respected and to have self-esteem and self-respect. Also known as the belonging need, this is the normal human desire to be accepted and valued by others. People need to engage themselves to gain recognition and have an activity or activities that give the person a sense of contribution, to feel accepted and self-valued, be it in a profession or hobby. Imbalances at this level can result in low self-esteem or an inferiority complex.

People with low self-esteem need respect from others. They may seek fame or glory, which again depends on others. Note, however, that many people with low self-esteem will not be able to improve their view of themselves simply by receiving fame, respect, and glory externally, but must first accept themselves internally. Psychological imbalances such as depression can also prevent one from obtaining self-esteem on both levels.

Most people have a need for a stable self-respect and self-esteem. Maslow noted two versions of esteem needs, a lower one and a higher one. The lower one is the need for the respect of others, the need for status, recognition, fame, prestige, and attention. The higher one is the need for self-respect, the need for strength, competence, mastery, self-confidence, independence and freedom. The latter one ranks higher because it rests more on inner competence won through experience. Deprivation of these needs can lead to an inferiority complex, weakness and helplessness.

Maslow also warns that even though these are examples of how the quest for knowledge is separate from basic needs, these 'two hierarchies are interrelated rather than sharply separated'. This means that this level of need, as well as the next and highest level, are not separate levels but are closely related to others. This is possibly the reason that these two levels of need are left out of most textbooks.

Self-actualisation

'What a man can be, he must be.' This forms the basis of the perceived need for self-actualisation. This level of need pertains to what a person's full potential is and realising that potential. Maslow describes this desire as the desire to become more and more what one is, to become everything that one is capable of becoming. This is a broad definition of the need for self-actualisation, but when applied to individuals the need is specific. For example one individual may have the strong desire to become an ideal parent, in another it may be expressed athletically, and in another it may be expressed in painting, pictures, or inventions. As mentioned before, in order to reach a clear understanding of this level of need one must first not only achieve the previous needs, physiological, safety, love, and esteem, but master these needs.

Maslow later added the level of 'Self-transcendence'.

The intelligence of laziness

It's no good just being lazy; you have to be better than lazy, you have to be lazy in a very smart way.

Productive laziness is not just about being lazy, it requires something more and that is a powerful and magical combination of laziness and intelligence. Smart lazy people have a real edge over others in society and are most suited to leadership roles in organisations.

This theory has existed for many years and has been applied in a number of interesting ways. One of the most famous of these was in the Prussian army.

Helmuth Karl Bernhard Graf von Moltke (1800–1891) was a German Generalfeldmarschall. The chief of staff of the Prussian army for thirty years, he is widely regarded as one of the great strategists of the latter half of the 1800s, and the creator of a new, more modern method, of directing armies in the field.

In 1857 Helmuth Moltke was given the position of Chief of the Prussian Großer Generalstab (military staff), a position he held for the next thirty years. As soon as he gained the position he went to work making changes to the strategic and tactical methods of the Prussian army: changes in armament and in means of communication, changes in the training of staff officers, and changes to the method of mobilising the army. He also instituted a formal study of European politics in connection with the plans for campaigns which might become necessary. In short, he rapidly put into place the features of a modern General Staff.

Moltke had a particular insight into and approach to categorising his officer corps, something which lives on to this day within many armed forces, and something which can apply to all forms of leadership.

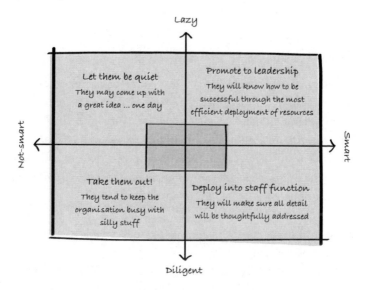

If you consider the two ranges of individual characteristics, those that go from diligent through to lazy, and those that go from non-smart through to smart (yes I am being politically correct here) then you end up with the four character types in the diagram above.

General von Moltke divided his officer corps into these four distinct types, depending on their mental and physical characteristics. He ended up with (and he never had to be politically correct being born in the nineteenth century and being chief of the Prussian army) the following types.

Type 'A' officers were mentally dull and physically lazy, were given simple, repetitive, and unchallenging tasks to perform. They had reached their career peak in the army. That said, if you left them alone then they might just come up with a good idea one day, if not then they wouldn't cause you any problems either.

Type 'B' officers were mentally bright and physically energetic. They were considered to be obsessed with micromanagement and would, as a result, be poor leaders. Promotion was possible over a period of time but not to the status of commanding officer of the German General Staff. These officers were best at making sure orders were carried out and thoughtfully addressing all the detail.

Type 'C' officers were mentally dull but physically energetic and were considered to be somewhat dangerous. To Moltke, they were officers who would require constant supervision, which was an unacceptable overhead and distraction, and because they would potentially create problems faster than could be managed, these officers were considered too much trouble and were dismissed. No career there then!

Type 'D' officers were the mentally bright but physically lazy officers whom Moltke felt could and should take the highest levels of command. This type of officer was both smart enough to see what needed to be done but was also motivated by inherent laziness to find the easiest, simplest way to achieve what was required. Put in a more positive way they would know how to be successful through the most efficient deployment of effort.

'Whenever there is a hard job to be done I assign it to a lazy man; he is sure to find an easy way of doing it.'

Walter Chrysler

129

So, smart lazy people have a real edge over others and are most suited to leadership roles in organisations.

It's a kind of magic: when one plus one equals so much more than two

What do you get when you cross one of the seven deadly sins with an accelerant for resource usage?

lazy [l'eɪzi]
adjective (lazier; laziest)

1. If someone is **lazy**, they do not want to work or make any effort to do anything.

Lazy and incompetent workers are letting the company down.

I was too **lazy** to learn how to read music.

- **laziness**   noun

Current employment laws will be changed to reward effort and punish **laziness**.

2. You can use **lazy** to describe an activity or event in which you are very relaxed and which you do or take part in without making much effort.

Her latest novel is perfect for a **lazy** summer's afternoon reading.

We would have a **lazy** lunch and then lie on the beach in the sun.

- **lazily**   adverb

Lisa went back into the kitchen, stretching **lazily**.

3. If you describe something as **lazy**, you mean that it moves or flows slowly and gently.

... a valley of rolling farms spread out along a **lazy** river.

- **lazily**   adverb

The river threaded its way **lazily** between the old city and the new.

Laziness – sloth: apathy and inactivity in the practice of virtue (personified as one of the deadly sins).

So lazy, or laziness, is mostly seen as a negative term, or at the very best, a term of selfish indulgence.

Productivity, on the other hand, is seen as a very positive term. The ratio of work produced in a given period of time, productivity relates to the person's ability to produce the standard amount or number of products, services or outcomes as described in a work description.

So, put the benefits of productivity together with an intelligent application of laziness and you get 'Productive laziness'.

Or to put it another way, you get the maximum output for any given input, with an eye to minimising the input as well. Or, to put it yet another way, you get a lot of bang for your bucks!

It's a Jungle (Book) out there!

Doo be doo be doo: Inspiration from a great 'character' actor.

You know that scene from *Jungle Book*, one of Disney's great films,[1] where the bear, Baloo, encourages Mowgli, the boy child, to think about life in a different way?

---

1. *The Jungle Book* is a 1967 animated feature film, released on 18 October 1967. The nineteenth animated feature in the Disney animated features canon, it was the last to be produced by Walt Disney, who died during its production. It was inspired by stories about the feral child Mowgli from the book of the same name by Rudyard Kipling. The movie remains one of Disney's most popular, and contained a number of classic songs, including 'The Bare Necessities' and 'I Wanna Be Like You'. Most of the songs are by Richard M. Sherman and Robert B. Sherman.

Baloo sings about looking for just the bare necessities of life, about trying to relax and cool it, and not spending any time looking for things that aren't worth it or can't even be found. Or, to put it another way, he is explaining to Mowgli that life using the good old 80/20 rule can be a lot less stressful.

For me 'The Bare Necessities' could well be the 'Productive lazy' theme tune. Check out the full lyrics some time, take a stroll down memory lane and watch the film one more time and enjoy Baloo the (singing) Bear teaching you all about the bare necessities of life that will come to you.

If that isn't good old doo be doo be doo productive laziness I don't what is!

The chicken or the egg

Scientists have finally cracked one of the world's oldest riddles – which came first, the chicken or the egg?

A supercomputer gave the team from Sheffield and Warwick Universities the answer – the chicken.

Apparently the discovery was a very happy accident. The original goal of the research was to find out more about how animals make eggshell. We underestimate chickens and we don't realise the amazing process they perform each time they make an egg. When you crack into your boiled egg in the morning, you are looking at one of the most amazing materials in the world. Eggshell is incredibly strong yet very lightweight. Humans can't get close to making anything like it.

But the problem is we just don't know how chickens make eggshell. They control this process in exquisite detail, yet we don't even know where to begin. Understanding how they build eggs would begin to tell us how we can do it ourselves.

The scientists turned to a super computer based in Edinburgh called HECToR (High End Computing Terascale Resource). They wanted it to figure out how eggs are built, by looking at the process in microscopic detail. First they programmed in the 'ingredients' that chickens use to make eggshells and then asked the computer to go and work it all out.

This computer worked on the problem for weeks and weeks, while a chicken, on the other hand, can do it pretty much overnight.

The results showed that a particular protein in chickens acts as a tireless builder, placing one microscopic section of shell on top of the other. It initiates this building process before going off to start on another part of the egg. Without this builder protein, the eggs would not exist. And yet it is only found in a chicken's ovaries.

This means the bird must have come first.

But where did the chicken come from?

I guess we are back to dinosaurs again.[2]

Six degrees of separation

No longer limited strictly to academic or philosophical thinking, this notion has recently become influential throughout popular culture. Further advances in communication technology – and particularly the Internet – have drawn great attention to social networks and human interconnectedness. As a result, many popular media sources have addressed the term.

Origins

American playwright John Guare wrote a play in 1990 and later released a film in 1993 that popularised it. It is Guare's most widely known work.

---

2. You'll need to read *The Lazy Project Manager* to understand this.

The play ruminates upon the idea that any two individuals are connected by at most five others. As one of the characters states:

'I read somewhere that everybody on this planet is separated by only six other people. Six degrees of separation between us and everyone else on this planet. The President of the United States, a gondolier in Venice, just fill in the names. I find it a) extremely comforting that we're so close, and b) like Chinese water torture that we're so close because you have to find the right six people to make the right connection... I am bound to everyone on this planet by a trail of six people.'

Guare, in interviews, attributed his awareness of the 'six degrees' to Marconi. Although this idea had been circulating in various forms for decades, it is Guare's piece that is most responsible for popularising the phrase 'six degrees of separation'. Following Guare's lead, many television and film sources would later incorporate the notion into their stories.

The game 'Six Degrees of Kevin Bacon' was invented as a play on the concept. The goal is to link any actor to Kevin Bacon through no more than six connections, where two actors are connected if they have appeared in a movie or commercial together.

Applications

SixDegrees.com was an early social-networking website that existed from 1997 to 2001. It allowed users to list friends, family members and acquaintances, send messages and post bulletin board items to people in their first, second, and third degrees, and see their connection to any other user on the site. At its height it had approximately one million users.

A Facebook platform application named 'Six Degrees' was developed by Karl Bunyan, which calculates the degrees of separation between different people. It had over 5.8 million users, as seen from the group's page. The average separation for all users of the application is 5.73 degrees, whereas the maximum degree of separation is 12.

Along the same lines was the group 'Six Degrees of Separation – The Experiment', which instructed new members to invite six people on their friend list, and is cited in a report about the theory. The group however, had no way to check if everyone is actually within six degrees of each other, and has since been deleted. However, a newer group with the same name revived the intent of the deleted group.

In 2008 Microsoft declared this concept was actually true. In a world of 6.6 billion people it seems hard to believe that you are just six introductions away from any other person on the planet, but Microsoft researchers announced the theory was right – nearly. By studying billions of electronic messages, they worked out that any two strangers are, on average, distanced by precisely 6.6 degrees of separation. In other words, putting fractions to one side, you are linked by a string of seven or fewer acquaintances to Madonna, the Dalai Lama and the Queen.

Researchers at Microsoft studied records of 30 billion electronic conversations among 180 million people in various countries, according to the *Washington Post*. This was 'the first time a planetary-scale social network has been available,' they observed. The database covered the entire Microsoft Messenger instant-messaging network in June 2006, equivalent to roughly half the world's instant-messaging traffic at that time.

The LinkedIn professional networking site operates on the concept of how many steps you are away from a person you wish to communicate with. The site encourages you to pass messages to people in your network via the people in your 1st-degree connections list, who in turn pass it to their 1st-degree connections.

TwitterUsers on Twitter can follow other users creating a network. According to a study of 5.2 billion such relationships by social media monitoring firm Sysomos, the average distance on

Twitter is 4.67. On average, about 50% of people on Twitter are only four steps away from each other, while nearly everyone is five steps away.

Nigel's other jokes

Nigel does like to share his sense of humour (that is what he describes it as anyway) and these are some of his other favourite jokes.

The innovative chicken (thinking outside the box)

A man was driving along a freeway when he noticed a chicken running alongside his car. He was amazed to see the chicken keeping up with him, as he was doing 50 mph. He accelerated to 60, and the chicken stayed right next to him. He sped up to 75 mph, and the chicken passed him. The man noticed that the chicken had three legs. So, he followed it down a road and ended up at a farm. He got out of his car and saw that all the chickens had three legs.

He asked the farmer 'What's up with these chickens?'

The farmer said 'Well, everybody likes chicken legs, so I bred a three-legged bird. I'm going to be a millionaire.'

The man asked him how they tasted.

The farmer said 'Don't know, haven't caught one yet.'

Moral: Be free in your thoughts but do think your plans all the way through to end.

Dealing with people (by confusing them)

A wise old gentleman retired and purchased a modest home near a junior high school. He spent the first few weeks of his retirement in peace and contentment. Then a new school year began.

The very next afternoon three young boys, full of youthful, after-school enthusiasm, came down his street, beating merrily on every trashcan they encountered. The crashing percussion continued day after day, until finally the wise old man decided it was time to take some action.

The next afternoon, he walked out to meet the young percussionists as they banged their way down the street. Stopping them, he said 'You kids are a lot of fun. I like to see you express your exuberance like that. In fact, I used to do the same thing when I was your age. Will you do me a favour? I'll give you each a dollar[3] if you'll promise to come around every day and do your thing.'

The kids were elated and continued to do a bang-up job on the trashcans. After a few days, the old-timer greeted the kids again, but this time he had a sad smile on his face.

'This recession's really putting a big dent in my income,' he told them. 'From now on, I'll only be able to pay you 50 cents to beat on the cans.'

The noisemakers were obviously displeased, but they accepted his offer and continued their afternoon ruckus. A few days later, the wily retiree approached them again as they drummed their way down the street.

'Look,' he said 'I haven't received my Social Security check yet, so I'm not going to be able to give you more than 25 cents. Will that be okay?'

'Only a quarter?' the drum leader exclaimed. 'If you think we're going to waste our time, beating these cans around for a quarter, you're nuts! No way, dude. We quit!'

And the old man enjoyed peace and serenity for the rest of his days.

Moral: When faced with difficulties plan your strategy well and play the long game.

---

3. Currency dilemma – in an aim to reach and not alienate a global audience what currency do I use? Pounds sterling or US dollars? And then again do I use 'trashcan' or 'dustbin' and 'check' or 'cheque'? – hell I will go with the joke as I found it. Feel free to adapt to your local taste.

Keeping it simple (and seeing the obvious)

The Lone Ranger and Tonto went camping in the desert. After they got their tent all set up, both men fell sound asleep.

Some hours later, Tonto wakes the Lone Ranger and says 'Kemo Sabe, look towards sky, what you see?'

The Lone Ranger replies 'I see millions of stars.'

'What that tell you?' asked Tonto.

The Lone Ranger ponders for a minute then says, 'Astronomically speaking, it tells me there are millions of galaxies and potentially billions of planets. Astrologically, it tells me that Saturn is in Leo. Time wise, it appears to be approximately a quarter past three in the morning. Theologically, the Lord is all-powerful and we are small and insignificant. Meteorologically, it seems we will have a beautiful day tomorrow. What's it tell you, Tonto?'

'You dumber than buffalo shit. It means someone stole the tent.'

Moral: Look for the obvious as this will often be what is required.

Financial planning (and battle of the sexes)

Dan was a single guy living at home with his father and working in the family business.

When he found out he was going to inherit a fortune when his sickly father died, he decided he needed to find a wife with whom to share his money. One evening, at an investment meeting, he spotted the most beautiful woman he had ever seen. Her natural beauty took his breath away.

'I may look like an ordinary guy,' he said to her, 'but in just a few years, my father will die and I will inherit his millions.'

Impressed, the woman asked for his business card and three days later, she became his stepmother.

Moral: Knowledge is power (and possibly women are much better at financial planning than men).

Logic (can be illogical)

A logician saves the life of a tiny space alien.

The alien is very grateful and, since she's omniscient, offers the following reward: she will answer any question the logician might pose. Without too much thought (after all, he's a logician), he asks: 'What is the best question to ask and what is the correct answer to that question?'

The tiny alien pauses.

Finally she replies 'The best question is the one you just asked; and the correct answer is the one I gave.'

Moral: Life (and aliens) can be confusing.

The half glass (more explanations)

We have already seen that:

One person might say 'It's half-full.' He is an optimist.

A second person might say 'It's half-empty.' He is a pessimist.

A third might say 'It's twice as big as it needs to be.'

Here are some more definitions:

The realist says the glass contains half the required amount of liquid for it to overflow.

The cynic wonders who drank the other half.

The school teacher says it's not about whether the glass is half-empty or half-full, it's whether there is something in the glass at all.

The professional presenter does not care if the glass is half-full or half-empty; he just knows that starting the discussion will give him ten minutes to figure out why his PowerPoint presentation is not working.

The ground-down mother of a persistently demanding five-year-old says 'Sweetheart, it's whatever you want it to be, just please let Mummy have five minutes peace and quiet.'

The inquisitive troublemaker wants to know what's in the glass anyhow. And wants the rest of it.

The worrier frets that the remaining half will evaporate by next morning.

The entrepreneur sees the glass as undervalued by half its potential.

The computer specialist says that next year the glass capacity will double, be half the price, but cost you fifty per cent more.

The logician says that where the glass is in process of being filled then it is half-full; where it is in the process of being emptied then it is half-empty; and where its status in terms of being filled or emptied is unknown then the glass is one in which a boundary between liquid and gas lies exactly midway between the inside bottom and the upper rim, assuming that the glass has parallel sides and rests on a level surface, and where it does not then the liquid/gas boundary lies exactly midway between the upper and lower equal halves of the available total volume of said glass.

The scientist says that a guess based on a visual cue is inaccurate, so mark the glass at the bottom of the meniscus of the content, pour the content into a bigger glass; fill the empty glass with fresh content up to the mark; add the original content back in; if the combined content overflows the lip, the glass was more than half-full; if it doesn't reach the top, the glass was more than half-empty; if it neither overflows nor fails to reach the top then it was either half-full or half-empty.

The grammarian says that while the terms half-full and half-empty are colloquially acceptable the glass can technically be neither since both full and empty are absolute states and therefore are incapable of being halved or modified in any way.

The waiter will hurry to replace it with a full one. For him there are no doubts: the glass was empty when he took it away; it is full in the bill that he brings you.

The magician will show you the glass with the full half at the top.

The physician says that the glass is not empty at all – it is half-filled with water and half-filled with air – hence, fully filled on the whole.

The ineffective organisation would discuss the question during a meeting of the board of directors, convene a committee to research the problem, and assign tasks for a root cause analysis, usually without a complete explanation of the problem to those assigned the tasks. The directors would consider the problem to be above the pay grade of those assigned root cause analysis tasks.

Peter Taylor

Introduction

Peter is a dynamic and commercially astute professional who has achieved notable success in business.

He is also an accomplished communicator and leader and is a professional speaker as well as the author of *The Lazy Project Manager* (Infinite Ideas) and *Leading Successful PMOs* (Gower).

More information can be found at www.thelazywinner.com

Speaking at your event

Peter can be persuaded to get out of his really comfortable chair if you feel the need to hear the benefit of his wisdom at your business event.

Want to find out more? Then just go to www.thelazywinner. com. There are workshops and training sessions around the 'lazy winning' theme if you really want to get 'lazy' fast.

Speaking references

'My expectations were high. I'm pleased to say that he delivered, in every sense of the word!'

'Entertaining public speaker and world-famous author... Peter has spoken at a number of events and has always been very well received. Highly recommend his book too! All this and a day job... read the book to find out how!'

'Peter gave a very entertaining and informative short presentation that left the audience wanting more.'

'Peter is a skilful speaker who fascinates his audience.'

'Peter has generated a hugely positive feedback following his presentations and I will not hesitate an instant to ask Peter to come back and mesmerise the us once again.'

'Peter showed a huge depth of knowledge and experience, was very engaging and explained his points with clarity and humour. The feedback we received from our members was extremely positive, and we would welcome having Peter present again at another of our events.'

'Peter is a self-effacing presenter poking fun at himself. All of this is what makes his presentation so good. If you are looking for a terrific presenter for your event, I highly recommend Peter.'

'His delivery style and content were instantly attention grabbing and audience feedback was excellent. I would thoroughly recommend Peter for other similar events.'

Peter's humorous and engaging style grabbed everyone from the moment he started until the very moment he stopped. If that's being lazy, then fantastic. I thought his energy levels were amazing. We were thrilled with Peter's performance.

Other books by Peter Taylor

The lazy project manager

The lazy project manager illustrates how anyone can apply the simple techniques of lazy project management in their own activities in order to work more effectively and consequently improve work–life balance. This 'productive laziness' approach builds on the Pareto principle that states that for many phenomena, eighty per cent of consequences stem from twenty per cent of the causes. To put it simply, only twenty per cent of the things people do during their working days really matter.

Inside this book readers can discover:

- The intelligence of laziness – why smart, lazy people have the edge over others.
- Why the *Jungle Book's* 'Bare Necessities' should be the productive lazy theme.
- How to get the maximum output for a minimised input.
- Quick tips to productive lazy heaven.

In addition, the author provides some interesting (and entertaining) information about eating dinosaurs, wearing ermine cloaks, and how to spot a psychopathic woman at a funeral. Also find out why you should never go ballooning, how to deliver a good Oscar acceptance speech, and why it is important for your team that you read the newspaper each morning.

And yes, you may also learn some, quick, simple but important things about project management.

Leading Successful PMOs

A PMO is a group or department within a business, agency or enterprise that defines and maintains standards for project management within the organisation. The primary goal of a PMO is to achieve benefits from standardising and following project management policies, processes, and methods. Over time, a PMO generally will become the source for guidance, documentation, and metrics related to the 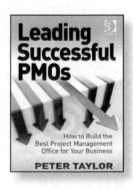 practices involved in managing and implementing projects within that organisation.

Summarising this then, a PMO should:

- Ensure that all projects are aligned with the overall business strategy.
- Highlight key project inter-dependencies and align releases across interdependent projects.
- Assist in timely decision making on the overall control of projects.
- Approve change requests of global relevance.
- Monitor and report projects.

Sounds simple perhaps, but in reality building an effective PMO is a complex process.

Leading Successful PMOs is a book to guide all project based organisations, and project managers who contribute to and benefit from a PMO (Project Management Office), towards maximising their project success.

'Find yourself a nice comfy chair, read this book and then take the lead in the introduction of a new order of things in your life, in a productive lazy way.'

The lazy winner, 2011

Index